Comm

Short Histories of Big Ideas Series List

Published   *Capitalism* Paul Bowles
                    Feminism June Hannam
                    Environmentalism David Peterson del Mar

Available soon *Fascism* Martin Blinkhorn
                    Nationalism Richard Bosworth
                    Zionism David Engel
                    Terrorism Rosemary O'Kane
                    Modernism Robin Walz

Communism

MARK SANDLE

PEARSON

Longman

Harlow, England • London • New York • Boston • San Francisco • Toronto
Sydney • Tokyo • Singapore • Hong Kong • Seoul • Taipei • New Delhi
Cape Town • Madrid • Mexico City • Amsterdam • Munich • Paris • Milan

PEARSON EDUCATION LIMITED

Edinburgh Gate
Harlow CM20 2JE
United Kingdom
Tel: +44 (0)1279 623623
Fax: +44 (0)1279 431059
Website: www.pearsoned.co.uk

First edition published in Great Britain in 2006

© Pearson Education Limited 2006

The right of Mark Sandle to be identified as author
of this work has been asserted by him in accordance
with the Copyright, Designs and Patents Act 1988.

ISBN-13: 978-0-582-50603-9
ISBN-10: 0-582-50603-4

British Library Cataloguing in Publication Data
A CIP catalogue record for this book can be obtained from the British Library

Library of Congress Cataloging-in-Publication Data
Sandle, Mark.
    Communism / Mark Sandle.
        p. cm. — (A short history of a big idea)
    Includes bibliographical references (p.) and index.
    ISBN-13: 978-0-582-50603-9
    ISBN-10: 0-582-50603-4
    1. Communism—History. 2. Communism—Soviet Union—History. 3. Soviet
Union—Politics and government. I. Title.

HX39.S234 2007
335.4—dc22

2006048550

10 9 8 7 6 5 4 3 2 1
11 10 09 08 07

Set by 35 in 9/15pt Iowan
Printed and bound in Malaysia

The Publisher's policy is to use paper manufactured from sustainable forests.

Contents

Series Editor's Preface

WHAT MAKES THE WORLD MOVE? Great men? Irresistible forces? Catastrophic events?

When listening to the morning news on the radio, reading our daily newspapers, following debates on the internet, watching evening television, all of these possibilities – and more – are offered as explanations of the troubles that beset the world in the Middle East, the 'war on terror' in Iraq and Afghanistan, environmental disasters at Chernobyl or New Orleans, and genocide in Sudan or Rwanda.

Where should we look to find answers to the puzzles of the present? To psychology? To economics? To sociology? To political science? To philosophy? Each of these disciplines offer insights into the personalities and the subterranean forces that propel the events that change the world, and within each of these disciplines there are experts who dissect current affairs on the foundation of these insights.

But all of these events, these problems, and even these disciplines themselves have one thing in common: they have a history. And it is through an understanding of the history of those ideas that inspired the people behind the events, and the ideas behind the ideologies that attempted to explain and control the forces around them that we can comprehend the perplexing and confusing world of the present day.

'Short Histories of Big Ideas' aims to provide readers with clear, concise and readable explanations of those ideas that were instrumental in shaping the twentieth century and that continue to shape – and reshape – the present. Everyone who attempts to follow the events of today via newspapers, television, radio and the internet cannot help but see or hear references to 'capitalism', 'communism', 'feminism', 'environmentalism', 'nationalism', 'colonialism' and many other 'isms'. And, while most of us probably believe that we have a basic understanding of what these terms mean, we are probably much less certain about who it was that coined, invented or defined them. Even more murky is our understanding of how these concepts moved from an idea to become an ideology and, perhaps, a phenomenon that changed the world. Most bewildering may be the disputes and controversies between factions and divisions within the movements and political parties that claim to be the true followers and the legitimate heirs of those who first conceived of the concepts to which they claim to adhere.

The authors of these Short Histories have been asked to write accessible, jargon-free prose with the goal of making comprehensible to the intelligent, interested but non-expert reader these highly complicated concepts. In each instance the approach taken is chronological, as each author attempts to explain the origins of these ideas, to describe the people who created them and then to follow the twisting path they followed from conception to the present. Each author in the series is an expert in the field, with a mastery of the literature on the subject – and a desire to convey to readers the knowledge and the understanding that the research of specialist scholars has produced, but which is normally inaccessible to those not engaged in studying these subjects in an academic environment.

The work of specialists often seems remote, obscure, even pedantic, to the non-specialist, but the authors in this series are committed to the goal of bringing the insights and understanding of specialists to a wider public, to concerned citizens and general readers who wish to go beyond today's headlines and form a more comprehensive and meaningful picture of today's world.

Gordon Martel
Series Editor

Timeline

1964	Khrushchev removed from power. Replaced by Brezhnev and Kosygin
1966	Cultural Revolution in China
1968	USSR invades Czechoslovakia
1973	Allende government overthrown in Chile
1975	Khmer Rouge come to power in Cambodia
	MPLA come to power in Angola
	Communist regime comes to power in Laos
1976	Death of Mao
1979	Overthrow of Pol Pot
1980	Strikes by Polish ship workers in Gdansk leads to Solidarity movement emerging
1982	Brezhnev dies. Replaced by Andropov
1984	Andropov dies. Replaced by Chernenko
1985	Chernenko dies. Replaced by Gorbachev. Start of reform of USSR
1989	Communist regimes collapse in Eastern Europe
	Revolt by students in Tiananmen Square
1991	Coup temporarily unseats Gorbachev
	USSR dissolved

Who's Who for *Communism*

Salvador Allende, 1908–73 Chilean communist leader.

Gracchus Babeuf, 1760–97 French radical political activist, precursor of 'modern' communism.

Leonid Brezhnev, 1906–82 Soviet leader from 1964–82.

Lev Davidovich Bronstein (Trotsky), 1879–1924 Russian revolutionary, theorist, writer. Murdered on Stalin's orders.

Nikolai Bukharin, 1888–1938 Russian Marxist and key theorist of early Bolshevism.

Etienne Cabet, 1788–1856 French utopian communist.

Tommaso Campanella, 1568–1639 Radical religious visionary, author of *Città del Sole* in 1602.

Fidel Castro, 1926– Cuban communist leader.

Iosif Vissionarich Djugashvili (Stalin), 1878–1953 Georgian revolutionary and head of the Soviet state.

Friedrich Engels, 1820–95 Factory owner, writer and close friend of Karl Marx.

Charles Fourier, 1772–1837 French philosopher and utopian dreamer.

Mikhail Gorbachev, 1931– Last leader of the USSR.

Antonio Gramsci, 1891–1937 Italian Marxist and revolutionary.

Enver Hoxha, 1908–85 Leader of the Albanian Communist state.

Nikita Sergeevich Khrushchev, 1894–1971 Soviet leader after Stalin.

John Lilburne, 1614–57 Agitator and pamphleteer during the English Civil War.

Karl Marx, 1818–83 Writer, philosopher and founder of 'modern' communism.

Jean Meslier, 1678–1733 Radical French cleric who advocated violent resistance and absolute egalitarianism.

Sir Thomas More, 1478–1535 Eminent politician and utopian philosopher, author of *Utopia*.

Thomas Münzer, 1489/90–1525 A religious radical in sixteenth-century Germany, leader of the German Peasants Rebellion.

Robert Owen, 1771–1858 Cotton manufacturer and creator of model community at New Lanark.

Pablo Picasso, 1881–1973 Radical artist, communist and activist in the peace movement.

Pol Pot, 1925–98 Leader of the Khmer Rouge in Cambodia until 1979.

Jean-Jacques Rousseau, 1712–78 French writer and philosopher, advocate of communal life.

Henri de Saint-Simon, 1760–1825 French writer and philosopher, advocate of technocracy.

Josip Broz Tito, 1892–1980 Yugoslav communist leader.

Mao Zedong, 1893–1976 Leader of the Chinese Communist Party.

Vladimir Ilych Ulyanov (Lenin), 1870–1924 Radical revolutionary, theorist and leader of the Russian Revolution.

Gerrard Winstanley, 1609–76 Activist and communalist radical during the English Civil War.

Acknowledgements

I SHOULD JUST LIKE TO acknowledge the help and support of a number of people, which has been crucial in this text finally seeing the light of day. Most of all thanks to Gordon Martel for his time, consideration and comments on the text at all stages, and his patience at points when it looked like it would never appear! Thanks are also due to my colleagues and students who over the years have played no little part in shaping my own thinking. Finally I need to thank my family – Wit, Luke, Beth and Cal – for putting everything in perspective. Wit, this one's for you. Still the one.

CHAPTER 1

A short introduction

Introduction

IN 1848 IN THE OPENING section of *The Manifesto of the Communist Party*, Marx and Engels wrote of 'a spectre . . . haunting Europe – the spectre of Communism' (Marx and Engels, 1848). Well, the spectre seems finally to have been laid to rest. Looking back over the history of communism, it seems strange to consider that it once haunted the establishment, lurking, waiting to pounce and turn the world upside down. At the peak of their power in the 1970s, communist parties held the reins across almost every continent. A few decades on, it now seems like something that belongs to another age. The years 1989 and 1991 saw communist parties felled and ushered ignominiously from power across Europe. With the rubble of the collapse of communism in the Soviet Union and Eastern Europe now being tidied away, with China rushing headlong to embrace capitalism, with increasing scepticism about big ideas and grand visions, and with communists increasingly marginalized in the industrialized North and West, many appear to believe that the time for writing communism's obituary is at hand.

In spite of the triumphalist outpourings of the heralds of capitalism, it is a little premature to write the obituary of communism. The forces and issues which led to the emergence of injustice, poverty, exploitation continue to cast a shadow over the world. The yearning for a better world still exists. Challenges to free-market capitalism and western liberal democracies continue to grow and spread. Critics of globalization, of consumerism, of environmental degradation constantly voice their concerns of the damage being done by twenty-first century capitalism. So, if an obituary is to be written perhaps it should be the obituary of the communist regimes and movements of the modern era (roughly 1840–1991) rather than the communist idea itself.

But the present does appear to be a good time to look back and review communism, both historically and philosophically. The demise of communist regimes allows us the opportunity to draw breath, and retrace the story. It is a fascinating story too, one which has much to say about who we are today, and how we have come to where we are. The story of communism is integral to understanding why the world is as it is today. Intriguingly, this story also offers us further insights into our current condition. Communism in its modern form emerged out of the profound social, economic, political and cultural disjunctures caused by the emergence of capitalism and the growth of industrialization in the early nineteenth century. There are many historical parallels with the current socio-political and economic shifts taking place in late capitalism, with the rise of postmodernism, biotechnologies, virtual technology and globalization. What can a reappraisal of communism tell us about how societies react when going through periods of extensive, deep-seated change?

What exactly do I mean when I say 'communism'? Communism has often been used interchangeably with other terms, most notably socialism. But although related, there is, conceptually and historically, clear blue water between the two. Communism is a clearly definable doctrine in its own right. Communism is a political movement and a socio-economic system on the one hand, and a set of ideas and theories on the other. This has led to disputes about the extent to which the communist movements and the communist regimes were actually 'communist'. Were those regimes really 'communist'? Or were they fundamentally perversions or distortions of the communist idea? Communism always acts as a critique of existing social, political, economic and cultural arrangements, and also offers an alternative to that reality, a vision of a radically different future. Yet the types of critique, and the forms of alternative have been very varied. Defining anything is a notoriously complex and rather slippery thing to engage in, but we have to start somewhere!

Generally speaking, a cluster of features and values can be identified as being part of the overall phenomenon of communism:

- a social system based on harmony, equality and cooperation;

- a collectivist or communal ethos or public morality;

- a socio-economic system based on holding property in common;

- the aspiration for a society which transcends individualism, competition, rivalry and selfishness;

- a utopian longing for a 'perfect' society which liberates humanity from its various forms of oppression.

The variety and diversity of communism can be explained by the way in which these values have combined and changed over the years, and by the context out of which they arose. Communism as a set of ideas and as a form of community organization can only fully be understood against the background of the particular society in which it grew, and in particular the specific oppression against which it was directed. Communist thinking about the future also has to be rooted in the society it emerged from and reacted against.

Writing about communism is a controversial business. Communism and, by extension, socialism were seen as being closely related to Stalinism, and so were to be rejected and attacked as oppressive ideologies which enslaved people. Supporters in turn denied that the Stalinist crimes had anything to do with communism. Instead, they argued that communist ideology was all about liberating people from the oppression of capitalism, not suppressing their freedom. The stakes have been raised recently. A number of books have tried to establish a clear and direct link between communism and terror, genocide and mass murder. The now notorious text *Le Livre Noir* (The Black Book) (Courtois, 1999) lifted the lid on the 'real' nature of communism. In a work that is part history, part polemic and part human ledger, Courtois *et al.* crunched the numbers of people killed under communist regimes:

- USSR: 20 million deaths;
- China: 65 million deaths;
- Vietnam: 1 million deaths;
- North Korea: 2 million deaths;

- Cambodia: 2 million deaths;

- Eastern Europe: 1 million deaths;

- Latin America: 150,000 deaths;

- Africa: 1.7 million deaths;

- Afghanistan: 1.5 million deaths;

- The international communist movement and communist parties not in power: about 10,000 deaths.

The total approaches 100 million people killed. One of the consequences of this type of approach has been to partially exonerate Nazism by claiming that it pales into insignificance when compared with the crimes of Stalinism (and so socialism/communism). One of the agendas behind this 'judgement of history' type approach has been to continue to discredit all left-wing ideas and ideals in the present, and so attempt to maintain the political hegemony of western liberalism. A little-noticed detail in the hullabaloo surrounding the publication of the Courtois tome was that one year later in 1998 Jean Suret-Canale published a *Black Book of Capitalism*, which presented a tally of victims far higher than that of communism. Its publication was almost totally ignored. The evils of communism are always, it seems, more newsworthy than the evils of capitalism.

The history of communism begins in earnest in the nineteenth century. But its roots go back much further in history.

Communism: the early years

No one is really sure where the term 'communism' actually originated from, although informed speculation suggests that it emerged in the early nineteenth century in Paris among revolutionary sects. Yet the nineteenth-century communist thinkers and movements were the heirs of a much longer tradition of speculative thought and organizational experimentation which might be grouped loosely under the term 'communist'.

Classical beginnings

Humankind has always deployed collectivist solutions to the economic, social, political and technological problems it has faced. The early origins of human society produced communal arrangements in response to the vagaries of the environment and the struggle to eke out an existence. Both nomadic communities and also pastoral and arable settlers organized their communities in such a way as to maximize the likelihood of group survival. This entailed organizing both production and distribution in such a way as to avoid risk and ensure that all members of the group or settlement were cared for. This communal/egalitarian structure was essentially a consequence of the low productivity and primitive levels of technical development of ancient human societies. However, this 'early' or primitive communism cannot really be considered as a genuine alternative to the existing forms of social organization. It was purely the most effective form of society at that time.

The first speculative philosophizing on a form of ideal society came from Plato in *The Republic*. Although Plato's vision was a deeply conservative one, and is not really a precursor of communist thinking, its utopian speculations can be likened to many other utopian dreamings. Unlike the Romans, the Greeks produced a more systematic corpus of writing and imaginings of a utopian ilk. Plato wrote of a future society which would be a Golden Age. This society was based on social stratification (including slavery) and divided society up into a rigid hierarchical class system: warriors, philosophers, commoners and slaves. But although this was a system of hierarchy it would provide the basis for a society of harmony as each person would occupy a place in the society which was appropriate to their interests. *The Republic* also asserted the need to remove the institution of private property as a precursor to a society of communal harmony.

Religious communism

The Middle East produced some of the earliest examples of radical, millenarian groups who sought to escape from the impurities and corruption of their societies. The Essenic communities grew up in the second century BC and combined a strict adherence to ceremonial religious regulations – celibacy, cleanliness, wearing white garments, and strict Sabbath observance – with egalitarian, communal and pacifist economic arrangements. The Essenes held their property in common, condemned slavery and prohibited trading as it promoted greed, cheating and covetousness. There was a strongly ascetic strand: embracing poverty as a virtue in its own right. A simple life, devoid of possessions was prized.

The emergence of the early Christian church in the first century AD saw a further mushrooming of communalism. Marx and Engels were clearly influenced by the experience of early Christianity in their theorizing about the nature of communism. The first century church committed itself to the common ownership of land, property, possessions so that all members of the community could be taken care of. There were limitations on the communal nature of the early church. They did not live in communal houses or in separate settlements. They essentially retained a familial basis to their social organization. Early Christianity rejected a society based on selfishness, greed and poverty. Instead they wished to model an alternative civilization based upon radical brotherhood, the sharing of wealth and possessions and the abolition of poverty among their brethren. They exhibited a profound indifference to personal property. This was not necessarily because they believed that personal property was itself intrinsically corrupt or evil. Instead, they believed fervently that everything they had belonged to God and they were merely stewards of this property. Moreover, their belief in the imminent return of Jesus Christ meant that they displayed a profound disregard for possessions. What use would possessions be in the hereafter?

The experiences of the early church provided a pattern which was adopted by a variety of Christian sects and monastic settlements. In the wake of a series of persecutions in the Roman Empire, many thousands of believers fled and began to form loosely based communities. The hardships they encountered may well have encouraged the adoption of ascetic and self-denying practices: celibacy and poverty in particular. These communities became the forerunners for the monasteries. It was Benedict in the early sixth century AD who provided the impetus for the growth of the monastic movement. Monasteries provided a retreat where individuals seeking spiritual salvation and purity could leave their society and live a life of simplicity, obedience, chastity and discipline. The individual subordinated their own needs and wishes fully to the life of the monastery and to God.

The motivation for these communities organizing their social, political and economic structures along collectivist, egalitarian and fraternal lines was the desire to pursue a different type of life. The reasons for choosing communal-type arrangements were many and varied. For some it was a religious imperative: a path of obedience, redemption, salvation. Others saw it as an economic imperative if the whole community was to survive. For many it was an opportunity to model an alternative way of living and an escape from a corrupt world. Perhaps the most significant thing to note at this point is that the elements which approximated most closely to communism in its 'modern' form – collective property, egalitarianism, social justice, cooperation, absence of hierarchy – were pursued at this point not as ends in themselves, but because they were seen as means to a higher goal. Whereas the communist movements of the nineteenth century sought to abolish the existing capitalist system and replace it *in toto* with something morally, economically, politically and socially superior, these 'early' movements sought instead to escape from the existing society. They dreamt of creating 'colonies of heaven' on earth.

Communism: medieval and early modern

The period from around the fourteenth century up until the seventeenth century saw a number of social and economic changes which produced a new wave of 'communist' speculations and experimentation. Life continued to throw up communities and social groups who found different ways of giving expression to communalist and cooperative ideas. In addition though, the Renaissance produced a proliferation of speculative utopian philosophizing. A variety of philosophers and commentators – including Thomas More, Tommaso Campanella, François Rabelais, James Harrington, Francesco Patrizi and others – created an array of different 'good societies', common to which were notions of communal property, egalitarianism and cooperative living and working.

Alongside the monastic model of communal living, there emerged a version of agrarian communism. The feudal manorial system had always deployed common cultivation of the fields and common rights to use grazing and woodland. From the mid fourteenth century onwards, climate change, the plague and rising population growth all combined to create economic problems. The onset of agrarian capitalism and the disputes over land ownership and tenure produced social tensions. A series of rebellions broke out across Europe. In Italy (1304–07), Flanders (1323–28), France (1356), England (1381), Northern Spain (1437), Bohemia (1419–34) and Hungary (1514) revolts and protests ignited the countryside. These popular uprisings of peasants and artisans often combined radical millenarianism with social protest. They turned to the Bible for an alternative way of living, and to endorse their critique of the existing elites and the distribution of land and power. Groups such as the Lollards in fourteenth-century England, the Hussites in Bohemia and the Flemish weavers all looked to create a society synthesizing radical Christianity and social reform. The most famous – and the one which is most often cited in histories of the growth of communism – was the Peasants Rebellion in Germany in 1525.

The central figure in the German Peasants Rebellion was Thomas Münzer, a religious radical who wanted to institute an egalitarian order in which all property was held in common. Although he was a strong advocate of social and economic justice, his views were aligned very closely to the radical religious movement of Anabaptism and were based upon his interpretations of the Bible. It was a synthesis of religious and agrarian communism. Münzer was highly critical of the obsession with the collection and possession of material things. He believed in holding all property in common, with its usage by individuals in accordance with their needs, and he believed in the radical egalitarianism of all Christians. He viewed the ordinary people as the victims of a system created by clerics and aristocrats for their own purposes. He wanted to liberate the people from the various forms of oppression – religious, social, economic – that they were experiencing. It is perhaps little wonder that Münzer is seen as a revolutionary role model by Marxists and radical socialists, although his essentially religious motivation for his economic and social prescriptions should be borne in mind. The Peasant Rebellion was to inspire further revolts in the years to come (Stayer, 1994).

Renaissance visions and dreams

The Renaissance produced a strand of more secular utopianism. In Germany, Italy and England the period between c. 1480 and c. 1620 saw a proliferation of utopian speculations, including those of Sir Thomas More (1478–1535) and Tommaso Campanella (1568–1639) among others. More's work *Utopia* was written in 1515 (More, 1989). *Utopia* was heavily influenced by Plato, and indeed More tended to view his work as the completion or fulfillment of Plato's *The Republic*, and so he explored many of the same themes, for instance about the freedom of the individual. *Utopia* was interestingly far more of an urban-based vision of the perfect society rather than the romantic rural idyll, with humanity living in harmony with each other and with nature.

The reason why More is often viewed as one of the precursors of modern communism is because he identified wealth and the lust for possessions as the root of all evil. However, this in many ways exemplifies the profoundly Christian nature of More's world-view. The reasons why there is conflict, tension and rivalry in society is because the accumulation of wealth and possessions makes individuals proud and arrogant and raises barriers between them. The solution put forward by More was to address the issue of wealth/property accumulation through a process of radical redistribution. More argued very strongly for a complete equality of property, to abolish monopolies of wealth, and also to ensure that there was no poverty in society. This would be reinforced by a rule involving labour for all, to prevent inequalities emerging.

Thomas More

More was a Londoner, born into a well-to-do family on 7 February 1478, the son of a prominent judge. His schooling took place at St Anthony's in London. A bright, articulate youth, he went to Oxford and studied Latin and logic under Thomas Linacre and William Grocyn. More decided to return to London in 1494 to study law, and he became a barrister in 1501. He was in two minds though about whether to pursue a career in the monastic orders, or whether to follow a calling into public life. After a brief sojourn in a Carthusian monastery, he decided to enter Parliament as an MP in 1504.

He married in 1505 (to Anne Colt who died in 1511) and they had four children. More was notable for providing a classical education for his daughters, something almost unheard of at the time.

More combined his political career with a prolific writing career. He quickly became recognized across Europe for his writing and he became good friends with and corresponded regularly with Erasmus of Rotterdam. In 1515 More wrote his most famous and controversial work, *Utopia*, a book in which a fictional traveller, Raphael Hythloday, describes the political arrangements of an imaginary island nation named Utopia. In the book, More contrasts the contentious social life of the Christian countries of Europe with the perfectly orderly and reasonable social arrangements of the non-Christian Utopia, where private property is absent and religious toleration is widely practised.

Having risen rapidly through the political hierarchy to become Lord Chancellor in 1530, More became increasingly uneasy at the religious reforms of Henry VIII and his disputes with the Pope. Henry became increasingly exasperated by More's opposition to his reforms. More was charged with treason in 1534 and beheaded. On the scaffold he declared that he died 'the king's good servant and God's first'. The execution took place on 6 July 1535. More's body was buried at the Tower of London, in the Church of St Peter ad Vincula. His head was placed over London Bridge for a month and was rescued by his daughter, Margaret Roper, before it was thrown in the Thames.

He was canonized by the Pope in 1935.

But it would be anachronistic and inaccurate to portray More as some kind of proto-communist, along with the monastic, mystics and agrarian rebels we have looked at up to this point. This is not to deny the clear intimations, hints and outlines of ideas which were developed in the 'modern' communism of the nineteenth and twentieth centuries. But the motivation and imperative behind these speculations was not the establishment of a communal or egalitarian society per se. The communal and egalitarian elements in More's utopia were designed as mechanisms to remove the primary problem bedevilling humanity: human arrogance and pride, the source of all sin.

Tommaso Campanella was an intellectually gifted, unorthodox and rebellious-minded monk from Calabria who lived, worked and wrote in a period of radical millennial visions and prophetic outpourings at the end of the sixteenth century. He is considered a forefather of communism, his name carved on an obelisk in Red Square as one of the forefathers of the Russian Revolution. A central context for understanding Campanella's work is his participation in a movement to liberate the republic of Calabria from Spanish overlordship. He was arrested and jailed between 1599 and 1626. During his incarceration, he wrote *City of the Sun (Città del Sole)* in 1602, a visionary account of a perfect community, riddled with messianic and prophetic themes, which aimed to abolish the family and private property (Campanella, 1981).

The *City of the Sun* would operate according to a series of radically egalitarian and communal principles. Those who laboured longest and hardest were deemed worthy of the most esteem and respect. Equality was achieved as everyone had everything they needed, and there was to be no accumulation of goods. At the heart of Campanella's vision though was the detail he provides of the communal life of the City. Citizens were brought up in communal dormitories. Women engaged in light labour, men in heavy labour. Children waited on tables. Men and women ate separately. Underpinning his vision was the central notion that

community, equality and communal living was a higher, superior and more authentically Christian form of social order.

Communism and the English Civil War

Rebellions, revolutions and popular uprisings often invoke utopian
speculation and social experimentation. The sense of 'turning
the world upside down', the release of energy, the feeling of
limitless possibilities all combine to create an atmosphere con-
ducive to radical change and innovative thought. In addition,
the post-revolutionary regime often assumes a dictatorial or
authoritarian shape, which itself provokes utopian thinking. The
English Civil War (1642–60) is cited by many as a key moment
in the development of proto-communist thinking, especially the
radical groups: Levellers, Diggers, Ranters. Each of these groups
issued a plethora of pamphlets, manifestos, tracts, blasts and
counter-blasts (Laslett, 1988).

It is important when viewing the works of the great pamphle-
teers and polemicists of this period – such as Gerrard Winstanley
and John Lilburne – to remember that, in spite of the radical
ideas, proposals and practices of these groups, the unifying
thread was essentially Christian and biblical. The inspiration was
the idea that the love of God for the poor and the needy required
a new type of society. With the rebellion against the Crown
under way after 1642, this prompted speculation about what
should rise up to take its place. Out of this poured a mighty
river of utopian thought and practice, much of which had a
communalistic dimension. Most of the visions were essentially
backward-looking; that is, they wanted to restore in England
some prior 'Golden Age'. Also, these were not universalist ideals,

but rather were addressed primarily at Englishmen. They shared a common set of enemies: nobles, royalty, clergy, lawyers and university scholars. Finally, the Bible provided the basis for the types of laws, social institutions and moral imperatives that should underpin the ideal society.

The Levellers were believed to be trying to 'level' everyone down through a policy of radical economic equality. This, however, is somewhat misleading. The reason why the Levellers are often included as proto-communists is because of their insistence on civil and political equality. The main leaders of the Levellers were John Lilburne, William Walwyn, Thomas Prince and Richard Overton. Their ideas originated from their experiences in the New Model Army, formed by Oliver Cromwell. Probably the best statement of Leveller beliefs was the 1649 manifesto *An Agreement of the Free People of England*. The thrust of the manifesto was to counter the imposition of arbitrary power, and so free the people from the oppression and injustice of the current state of affairs. In particular the manifesto sought to create a world of equality, prosperity, harmony and peace. The aim was a society without enmity or bitterness, discord or strife, in which each lived according to their own conscience, freed from oppression and burdens. There was no sense of communal property or collective labour in their political philosophy. Instead, they sought to highlight the political and social structures which could create a society free from oppression.

The Diggers were a more radical grouping than the Levellers. They were egalitarians, pacifists and communalists who wished to undertake a 'root and branch' restructuring of English economic and social structures. Their main spokesperson was Gerrard Winstanley (1609–76), a cloth merchant born in Wigan, whose business had been ruined by the war. In 1649 while in Surrey taking care of his friend's livestock, Winstanley had a mystical revelation in a vision. In this vision (a commonplace among prophets and millenarian visionaries) he was commanded to gather to himself a community and dig up and plant the common land and live on the produce. He obeyed the commanding voice. In April 1649, he and 20–30 others set about cultivating a patch of common ground on St George's Hill near Cobham in Surrey, and inviting others to come and join them. This practice would help to alleviate the severe poverty of the ordinary people. It was deeply contentious because it infringed the property rights of local landlords and provoked a violent reaction from the landowners, and, by Easter 1650, the Digger colony had been eradicated.

Winstanley outlined his ideas in a number of tracts, *A Declaration from the Poor, Oppressed People of England, The True Levellers Standard Advanced*, and *A Letter to the Lord Fairfax and His Councell of War* (all 1649) (Hopton, 1989). His last work, *Law of Freedom* (1652) argued forcefully that all the laws and institutions of England should be revised immediately in order to bring social and economic equality to all men through the common ownership and cultivation of the land. On many occasions he talked of the need to abolish buying and selling, fairs and markets. In one pamphlet he stated that, 'For the earth, with all her Fruits of Corn, cattle and such like, was made to be a common store-house of livelihood to all mankind, friend and foe without exception' (Hopton, 1989: 76).

Thus under Winstanley's new world, money is abolished, and all produce is taken to commonly owned storehouses from which all families will draw their supplies. Health care is also free. The links with subsequent radical communists and their critique of capitalism, private property, the market and such are evident. Yet it would be wrong to overstate this. Winstanley's ideas and ideals were clearly underpinned by radical Christian beliefs, and his lists of virtues and vices were ones drawn from the Puritan tradition. The vices of society were covetousness, injustice, anger, promiscuity. Virtues were selflessness, purity, justice and tenderness. The good society was one of cooperation, harmony, justice and altruism. But it was a society with a strongly authoritarian and punitive streak. This was not to be a loose, self-governing commune. It was a highly regulated society of supervisors, overseers and magistrates all in place to ensure that people did not lapse back into idleness or covetousness. Children were to be socialized through education. Dissenters and the disobedient were to be physically punished. Labour was compulsory to prevent the lazy and the indolent unfairly exploiting the others. Anyone caught buying and selling would be executed. Everyone would be forced to learn a craft and would have to retire at forty. Loafing or parasitism would result in slavery. Although there were many other significant groups – including Ranters and the Fifth Monarchists – it was the Levellers and the Diggers who provided the subsequent inspiration for later communist thinkers and theorists. This combination of radical thinking, savage criticism of an unjust present, and practical direct action aimed at dispossessing the ruling elites and empowering the masses to confront their oppressors all served as inspiration for 'modern' communists. This though should not disguise the fact that, even in the 1640s and 1650s, these thinkers were essentially 'backward looking' (seeking to restore a lost golden age), primarily motivated by religious/Christian ideals and were usually the result of one man's thoughts and dreams.

Gerrard Winstanley

Gerrard Winstanley was born in Wigan, Lancashire, in 1609. He was the son of a grocer. In 1637 he moved to London where he became an apprentice and eventually a member of the tailors' guild. In September 1640 Winstanley married Susan King and they were forced to move back to Lancashire by the Civil War, which disrupted his work.

Winstanley's first important tract was entitled *The New Law of Righteousness*. In it he set out a vision of society which could be termed Christian communism, and which accounts for his place in the pantheon of communist thinkers. Winstanley took various portions of the Bible – the equality of all people, mistrust of kings, common ownership of property by the early church – to advocate a radical social set-up which abolished private property and the aristocracy.

Winstanley was not just a pamphleteer, he was also an activist. He created a group known initially as the 'True Levellers' but eventually known as the 'Diggers' because of their activities. In April 1649, Winstanley and about thirty followers settled on the common land of St George's Hill in Surrey to establish *free communism*. They distributed crops free of charge to their followers. Diggers also took over land in other places in England to the great annoyance of landowners. Soon, hired thugs were attacking the Digger settlements. It took a year before all Diggers had resigned or were killed. They received no protection from the authorities.

In 1660 Winstanley moved to Cobham in Surrey and became a Quaker and worked as a cloth merchant in London until his death in 1676.

Between the English Civil War and the French Revolution (1789), there were a handful of philosophers who advanced ideas about collectivism and communalism. In the latter half of the eighteenth century, some theorists speculated that the natural condition of society must have been one of collective rather than private ownership. Among them were Thomas Raynal, Jean Meslier, Gabriel de Bonnot de Mably, Simon Linguet and Morelly. One of the most intriguing of the writers of this time (most of whom were clerics or religious figures) was the Curé Jean Meslier. Meslier was born in 1678, the son of a serge-weaver, and later became parish priest of Etrepigny in the Ardennes. A consistent defender of the rights of his peasant parishioners, Meslier led a life of personal austerity. In terms of the origins of communism, Meslier advocated radical egalit-arianism, and believed in violent resistance and rebellion as a means of achieving his goals (Carey, 1999). Morelly (subse-quently cited by both Babeuf and Marx) also advocated a social system based on fraternalism, communalism and egalitarianism. He outlined a detailed constitution that would enable agrarian societies to live sociably and peacefully. This encompassed the abolition of private property, which was seen as the key to regen-erating the family.

Rousseau, The French Revolution and Babouvism

The bridge between pre-modern and modern communism was sketched by the philosophy of Jean-Jacques Rousseau, con-structed during the French Revolution and first crossed by François Nöel (aka 'Gracchus') Babeuf's movement, the Con-spiracy of Equals. Rousseau's writings grappled with many of the key ideas which were to surface in later communist theories, most notably of how to create a society which reconciles the individual and the collective, which enables a synthesis of the human imperatives for personal identity and communal belonging. Rousseau's writings echoed earlier writings in that he pointed back to a lost 'Golden Age', a rural idyll of lost innocence, simplicity, purity, and proximity to and harmony with nature (Cranston, 1991; 1999). Rousseau's work attempted to describe the creation of a holistic collective. Where Rousseau stands apart from his proto-communist predecessors is that he does not argue for absolute equality, and is little concerned with the questions of property ownership. Instead in his concern to spell out how the good society might set about reconciling the individual with the collective, he wrestles with one of the key aspects of 'modern' communist thinking. But Rousseau does not just prefigure later theoretical debates, he also had a more direct impact upon the development of the communist ideal, through his radical followers: Babeuf and Saint-Just.

Babeuf was born in 1760, and was executed in 1797 by the French authorities because of his conspiratorial activities. He was born in the countryside in Picardy. He became a minor clerk in the French provincial administration, and was given the job of overseeing the archives and transactions of the feudal estates, giving him first-hand knowledge of the abuses and inequalities of the feudal system. He had a deep hunger to learn and improve himself, and so he read the works of the French *philosophes* avidly, including of course Rousseau. The first inkling of his radical views came in the period after 1785 in his correspondence with Dubois de Fosseux, who was secretary of the Academy of Arras (Rose, 1978).

Babeuf's first foray into openly revolutionary activities took the form of local protest against tax increases and led to participation in and leadership of local movements which aimed to highlight what were quite populist causes. He moved between the capital and the provinces, and became increasingly outspoken and critical through pamphlets and brochures that attacked injustice. Babeuf also became a revolutionary in action, not just in word. Drawn into the world of revolutionary agitation, he began to work openly for a form of government and social structure which would create equality, and eliminate suffering, poverty and misery for the masses. In 1795, along with Sylvain Marechal and Filippo Buonarotti, he formed the Conspiracy of Equals, who were dedicated to bringing down the Directory and installing a new radically egalitarian regime. In his writings, which were discovered when he was arrested and his plot uncovered, we see a programme which contains the first inklings of the emergence of a new form of communism, and a new rationale for its implementation.

Although Babeuf's views were influenced by the agrarian communism of Morelly, Mably and others, and also harked back to the communistic patterns of Sparta, his advocacy of equality has a distinctly 'modern' feel to it, pointing towards Marx. Babeuf elaborated his views in *The Doctrine of Babeuf*. The key guarantors of an egalitarian society were property, work and education. Babeuf believed that nothing should be allowed to transgress the principle of absolute equality. One person should not have more of one item than another person. If so, the item itself should be outlawed. This was to be underpinned by the production of an abundance of the necessity items in a society, and by very few luxury items. Only in this way could shortages be prevented, one of the key factors in the creation of inequality. But for this to work, this meant a society had to be created which moderated expectations and desires, in order that people should be content with necessities, and not yearning for luxuries. This required a highly disciplined community (either self-discipline or imposed from outside) of self-denying, altruistic people.

In terms of labour, this was an expectation and an obligation for all. There was no room for slackers, shirkers and the downright lazy. But labour itself would be transformed into something pleasurable, or at least non-onerous. Incentives to work were premised upon patriotism, public-spiritedness and gratitude. Education was seen as critical in bringing about a society which could actually provide for the welfare of all. Babeuf saw the equal distribution of knowledge as a crucial guarantor in making people equal in capacity and talent, and so removing the foundations of the whole edifice of inequality in society. This social system was potentially a highly authoritarian one: individual distinctions and differences would be forcibly crushed to ensure equality. Boredom and inactivity were to be driven out by a highly planned series of public activities. Labour and the distribution of its fruits would be both compulsory and organized by the state. It was also a society designed specifically for the welfare of the community, not the individual. But the final outcome was to be a society free from despair, worry, misery and insecurity. Unfortunately, Babeuf was never able to realize his dream: he was guillotined on 27 May 1797 along with his fellow conspirator Darthe.

Babeuf's contribution to the history of communism is highly significant. He marks the transition between the earlier forms of agrarian/religious communism and the industrial and 'modern' communism of the nineteenth century and beyond. His writings, mentality and principles point backwards and forwards. His vision is essentially an agrarian one, but it also contains an awareness of the problems being created by the shifts to urban living and industrial manufacture. His vision is in many ways quite secularized: he sees equality and a communal life as good things in themselves rather than as things which may usher in the Kingdom of God. His primary thrust was the here and now, not the hereafter. He did not argue for a simple lifestyle based on necessity on the grounds that it reflected the heartbeat of the Christian message, but because that was the most effective way to ensure equality and the welfare of all. He also at times looked back to classical civilization for his inspiration.

Gracchus Babeuf

François Babeuf was born in Saint-Quentin on 23 November 1760. He grew up in a materially impoverished household. Before the French Revolution he was employed as a *commissaire à terrier* at Roye, a position in which he was supposed to help the landed aristocracy assert their feudal rights over the peasants. He started to write regularly in the late 1780s, usually on literary topics, although early signs of his socialist leanings can be detected. In 1789, on the eve of the Revolution, he wrote the section of the petition from the village of Roye which requested the king to abolish all feudal rights.

In the early years of the Revolution, Babeuf held minor government posts in Somme, in Montdidier, and finally in Paris, where he settled in 1793. In 1794 he began to publish the *Journal de la liberté de la presse*, later known as *Le Tribun du peuple*. In an article written shortly after the Thermidorian coup, Babeuf expressed radical democratic ideas. At this time he began to call himself Caius Gracchus Babeuf, after the Roman social reformer.

In October 1794 Babeuf was arrested for attacking the government's economic policies. After his release the following year, he became one of the Directory's most violent critics. In *Le Tribun du peuple* he put forth his socio-economic ideas and called for the establishment of a republic of equals. He declared that the government was comprised of 'starvers, bloodsuckers, tyrants, hangmen, rogues and mountebanks'. He soon attracted a following of former Jacobins, and they opened a club at the Panthéon. In February 1796 the government closed the club and planned to take actions against the group, which was becoming a political menace.

Meanwhile, Babeuf and his supporters were plotting an attack upon the government. They wanted to implement the Constitution of 1793, because they believed that it would place governmental power in the hands of the people. Their movement – dubbed 'The Conspiracy of Equals' – was set for a coup on 10 May 1796. However, their plan was betrayed by the spy Georges Grisel, and on 10 May Babeuf and the other leaders (including Alexander Darthe and Philippe Buonarotti) of the movement were arrested. On 26 May 1797, Babeuf was condemned to death and he was executed the next day.

Babeuf also points forward to the emergence of radical, uncompromising communist political movements. He grapples with one of the questions that dominated communism in the nineteenth century: how can a communist system be realized in practice? Babeuf represents one of the forerunners of the uncompromising school: 'it is indubitable that this change could be brought about except by the overthrow of the established government and the suppression of everything in the way.' He also prefigures debates about whether communism should be established primarily through the actions of a dedicated elite, or by the masses themselves.

Conclusion

Communism and communalist ideas have a long historical pedigree. The aspiration to create a society based on equality, harmony, fraternity and cooperation has found expression in many different cultures and contexts. Communist ideas prior to the modern industrial world were usually inspired either by radical religious thought or by classical ideals. On this basis, communal forms of property ownership, egalitarian social structures, communities based on harmony and cooperation were either inspired by a sense of radical social justice (to alleviate the suffering of the poor and downtrodden) or by the aspiration to lead a life based on simplicity and necessity in imitation of the early apostles. Equality and social justice were not seen as ends in themselves, but as means to the attainment of some spiritual or religious goal. These communalistic experiments or dreams were often the result of a profound sense of crisis, or socio-political disjuncture in the life of a society. Radical change, dislocation and shock provoked individuals to think, dream and create new, better, fairer ways of organizing society. Early communist thinkers were either backward-looking (seeking to restore some lost Golden Age) or were millenarian (looking to a coming age of divinely ordered harmony and peace). Little was written about creating this type of society in the here and now.

Finally, communism was either a series of ideas or fantastical visions emanating from the mind of philosophers or visionaries, or a small-scale local experiment. Little if any thought was given to the question of how you might get from the present to the communist society. Those who speculated on paper talked only of what the society might look like and how it might work.

Those who experimented by creating alternative ways of living, working and sharing did little more than set up small enclaves within the existing society as models of how it might be done differently. In this period, there was no sense (at least until Babeuf) of forging a movement to overthrow and remake society along communist lines. As the industrial era dawned, as the era of the nation-state with increased communications and contact between town and country began to unfold, so communist thinkers became more extensive in their thinking (that is, looking at ways to remake society *in toto* either on a national or an international scale), and also became increasingly concerned with the question of how to get from A to B.

Recommended reading

There are very few surveys of the whole sweep of communism. There has been a short introduction by Richard Pipes, *Communism* (Phoenix, 2002). Most of the other works have primarily been concerned with communism in its 'modern' form. The main works which provide a good, concise introduction to utopian thought and speculation include: John Carey (ed.), *The Faber Book of Utopias* (Faber and Faber, 1999); F.E. Manuel and F.P. Manuel, *Utopian Thought in the Western World* (Belknap Press, 1979). For details on the early communist practices of various groups and societies, see H. Chadwick, *The Early Church* (Penguin, 1967); M. Dunn, *The Emergence of Monasticism: From the Desert Fathers to the Early Middle Ages* (Blackwell, 2002); I. Bradley, *The Celtic Way* (Longman & Todd, 1997).

For developments during the English Civil War, see P. Laslett, *The World We Have Lost* (Routledge, 1988); F. Brockway, *Britain's First Socialists: The Levellers, Agitators and Diggers of the English Revolution* (Quartet, 1980); A. Hopton (ed.), *Gerrard Winstanley: Selected Writings* (Aporia Press, 1989). For writings on Jean-Jacques Rousseau, see the three volumes written by Maurice Cranston: *The Early life and Work* (University of Chicago Press,

1991); *The Noble Savage* (1999); *The Solitary Self* (1999). The best pieces on Babeuf include R.B. Rose, *Gracchus Babeuf: The First Revolutionary Communist* (Arnold, 1978); I. Birchall, *The Spectre of Babeuf* (Palgrave, 1997). To read Babeuf, visit the Marxist Internet archive www.marxists.org.

CHAPTER 2

The rise of 'modern' communism

Introduction

THE ROOTS OF TWENTIETH-CENTURY communism can be found in the nineteenth century. The French Revolution and the Babouvist movement mark the transition from the 'early' communism to the 'modern' form of communism, shaped primarily by Marx, Engels *et al*. The monumental impact of events in France between 1789 and 1799, and the onset of industrialization and urbanization in Great Britain and continental Europe provoked a series of widespread and often violent upheavals across Europe and beyond: economically, socially, politically, philosophically and culturally. In common with the periodic appearance of utopian communalist thinking prior to 1789, communist thinking in the nineteenth century arose out of a period of crisis and upheaval. This took many forms: theoretical speculations, pamphleteering, political agitation, and the creation of new communities built along co-operative lines. Communism developed alongside the growth of industrial society, as both moral criticism and political nemesis. One of the distinctive features of 'modern' communism was that it was more than just a set of doctrinal speculations or localized communal experiments. It was to become a full-scale political movement challenging the existing order in its entirety.

Marx and Engels clearly stand out as central figures in the development of communism as both a political doctrine and a political movement. Their views are best understood not just in terms of the logic of their own development, but also as arising out of debates with their contemporaries: people like Fourier, Saint-Simon, Owen, Sismondi, Cabet, Proudhon, Blanqui and others (Taylor, 1982).

The emergence of communism and socialism after 1789

The period between 1789 and *c.* 1850 was an extremely fertile time, ideologically speaking. The age of modern ideologies had dawned: liberalism, nationalism, socialism and communism all made their first appearances on the political stage (Hobsbawm, 1992). The emergence of capitalism, the demise of feudalism and the rise of economic individualism provided the impetus for the growth of ideologies critical of these new developments: socialism and communism. The extension of economic exploitation, poverty, wage labour and the division of labour encouraged a sense of rebellion against injustices and inequalities. How though can we distinguish between socialism and communism?

If we take the ideological spectrum at this point, then it would look something like this:

Liberalism---------------socialism---------------communism

Socialism bridges the divide between liberalism and communism, sharing some elements with both ideologies. By highlighting what was shared and what was unique about these different ideals, it becomes possible to identify the broad contours of communism as it emerged at this time. The basic starting-point was the attitude towards the newly emerging industrial system. Although critical of liberalism and capitalism, in its early stages socialism accepted industrialization but was critical of the particular form it had taken. It had become too individualistic and exploitative. The early socialists aspired to the reform of capitalism, through humane legislation and enlightened government (Lichtheim, 1975).

Both socialism and communism shared a critical attitude towards capitalism and liberalism. However, whereas the early socialists only went so far as to advance a moral critique of capitalism's excesses and injustices, communism's starting-point was this moral line, and developed into a wholesale critique of industrial society. What distinguished socialism and communism then was the critique offered of capitalism, the alternative put forward to capitalism and the means of expressing their protest and achieving their aims. The distinctive aspects of the communists were their radical egalitarianism (a trait inherited from the Babouvists), their predominantly proletarian make-up, and their revolutionary means to achieve their aims, rather than peaceful and piecemeal reforms. The aim of the communists was to overturn rather than reform society.

Communists and socialists: the French, British and Germans to 1847

The countries that produced most of the early examples of socialist and communist thinking were France and Great Britain (Germany joined in a little later). There are good reasons for this. Both countries were experiencing profound change. The spread of the industrial revolution from Britain to Belgium and France and the emergence of a proletariat saw the first inklings of social conflict and protest. The restoration of the Bourbon monarchy in 1815 and the subsequent July Revolution in 1830 in Paris signified the rise of liberalism in Europe, and provoked reactions against the individualism which it seemed to be advancing. But the responses to this situation were numerous and diverse, including philosophical speculation, the creation of communalist settlements and ideal communities, secret conspiratorial societies and revolutionary movements.

The figures most often seen as 'utopian socialists' rather than communists include thinkers and activists like Henri de Saint-Simon (1760–1825), Charles Fourier (1772–1837) and Robert Owen (1771–1858) among others (Taylor, 1982). As noted above, what united these thinkers was a desire to reform and improve the social and economic conditions in which people lived and worked, and generally they eschewed involvement in politics. They sought structures and organizations which would promote the happiness and welfare of individuals rather than the competitive, individualistic world of capitalism and liberalism. Their vision was to create a world free of dynastic conflict, social strife and poverty, a world of international peace and collaboration. But there were significant differences between them.

Saint-Simon was an interesting figure. Although he is often classified among the socialists, much of his thought is not specifically socialist. His underlying approach was to promote the welfare and well-being of the people through extolling the virtues of large-scale organization and scientific planning. His work *Le Nouveau Christianisme* (*The New Christianity* 1825) attempted to fuse fraternalism and science to create a society of fairness and rationality. Bankers and financiers would be mobilized to take control of nation-states and so transform them into great productive corporations, linked together in a world-wide network. Saint-Simon's vision – technocratic, industrial, technological, transnational – aimed to produce social harmony (Saint-Simon, 1975).

Owen and Fourier had very different visions from Saint-Simon and his followers (Kolakowski, 1978). They were essentially community-builders. They were animated by the desire to create an international network of local communities based on sociable and cooperative principles. They would overcome the competitive individualism of industrial society not by struggle or conflict, but by demonstrating the evident superiority of the communal life. Robert Owen was a successful cotton manufacturer who moved to New Lanark in Scotland and set up a model community: good housing, proper sanitation, non-profit stores and excellent educational opportunities. The spread of his ideas led to the formation of communities based on his principles, the most famous of which was founded in New Harmony in Indiana in 1825, but which sadly fell apart owing to internal dissensions not long after (Royle, 1998).

Fourier, a somewhat unorthodox figure, developed his idea that social harmony could be achieved if people were given the opportunity to pursue their passions. To enable this he set up social organizations called 'phalanxes', an economic unit comprised of 1,620 people. People would live in communal buildings, and would work according to their natural inclinations. The phalanstery would combine both industrial and agricultural work, and would operate on a cooperative basis. Inequality and private property would not be eliminated, but would be rendered non-antagonistic. Between 1841 and 1859 about 28 colonies were set up in the USA along the lines set out by Fourier (Kolakowski, 1978). In spite of the obvious differences between them, these early or utopian socialists shared many ideas. They were all opposed to individualism, laissez-faire and competition. Instead they wished to promote cooperation, the production and distribution of wealth to benefit all, and the importance of education as a means of creating sociable citizens and harmonious societies. Within their doctrines, there was no call for the abolition of private property, radical egalitarianism or class struggle. This provides the dividing line between the socialists and the communists in this period.

Perhaps the main figure who straddles the divide between the utopian socialists and the communists was Etienne Cabet (1788–1856) (Johnson, 1974). Cabet developed a theory of communism in his book *Voyage en Icarie*, which depicted an ideal society in which an elected government controlled all economic affairs and in which all things were held in common. Cabet's followers, who became known as Icarians, set up ideal communities in the USA in the 1840s. 'Communism' as a concept began to circulate in France in the ferment created after the 1830 revolution, but emerged in the 1840s to designate those groups who adhered to the views of Cabet. At this point, the term had a number of connotations, particularly within France. The term communism invoked both the notion of the 'commune': a decentralized, local self-governing form of social organization, and also 'community': a group of people sharing all things in common. In opposition to the socialists, the 'communists' emphasized revolution, militancy, class struggle and radical egalitarianism.

The origins of communism as an organized movement which emphasized and propagated these themes can be traced to the 1830s (Cole, 1958). In 1836 in Paris a small group of German exiles formed the League of the Just, dedicated to carrying on the Babouvist tradition of revolution and radicalism. Members of this group were involved with an insurrection in Paris in May 1839, led by August Blanqui, a radical figure who harked back to the revolutionary tradition of the Jacobins. When this attempted coup failed, the League of the Just was broken up and disappeared underground. The communist flame was kept alive in the cities of London, Brussels and Paris by workers' educational societies. Moves to link these different groups together into an international organization began in the early 1840s. Josef Moll travelled from London to Brussels to enlist the help of Karl Marx and Friedrich Engels. In the summer of 1847, a meeting took place to set up a League of Communists, which would in the first instance be German but which would become international in the long run. It was also decided that the League needed a manifesto. This task was entrusted to Marx. It was completed, with Engels, by January 1848, just as revolution broke out across continental Europe in that most momentous of years.

Before turning to look in some detail at the ideas of Marx and Engels, it is worth pausing to summarize what we have learnt so far about communism and the communist movement. In

addition to notions of radical egalitarianism, communal ownership and distribution to the benefit of the masses, communism
was revolutionary, militant, not averse to the use of violence and
committed to a class-based struggle for power. Communists
were not just more radical in the economic sphere, they were
also far more committed to the struggle for political power, to
direct action in the political arena, unlike the socialists at this
time who wanted to work for the peaceful, long-term transformation of society. Communists wanted to overturn the
existing distribution of power and wealth. The year 1848 seemed
to suggest that just such a confrontation was in the offing.

Karl Marx

Karl Marx was born in Trier, in the German Rhineland, on
5 May 1818. Although his family was Jewish they converted to
Christianity so that his father could pursue his career as a lawyer
in the face of Prussia's anti-Jewish laws. A precocious schoolchild,
Marx studied law in Bonn and Berlin, and then wrote a PhD thesis
in Philosophy, comparing the views of Democritus and Epicurus.
On completion of his doctorate in 1841 Marx hoped for an
academic job, but he had already fallen in with too radical a group
of thinkers and there was no real hope. Turning to journalism
Marx rapidly became involved in political and social issues. In
1843, Marx married Jenny, at Kreuznach, a childhood friend he
had become engaged to while still a student. They were to have
six children in all, although only three – Jenny, Laura and Eleanor
– were to survive into adulthood. The deaths of his children –
most notably his son Edgar in 1855 – profoundly affected Marx.

In September 1844, Frederick Engels came to Paris for a few
days, and from that time on became Marx's closest friend. Shortly
after meeting, Marx and Engels worked together to produce the
first mature work of Marxism – *The German Ideology*. As a result of
his revolutionary activities, Marx was banished from various

cities, moving from Paris to Brussels to Paris to Cologne to Paris and finally to London in 1849 where he lived until his death. Marx and his family lived in dire poverty for their initial time in London, supported by Engels' money. Money from his articles for the American press helped to alleviate the poverty somewhat. But the speed of Marx's writing and research in London was constantly hampered by the financial and emotional difficulties of his domestic life.

Marx played a key role in the fashioning of the International Working Men's Association in 1864. He worked exhaustively and exhaustingly in the 1860s and 1870s on *Capital* and analyses of the Civil War in France. His health began to deteriorate in the mid 1870s, and he was unable to complete the last two volumes of *Capital*. His wife died on 2 December 1881. In January 1883 his eldest daughter Jenny died at the age of 38. The shock of her demise hastened Marx's own death on 14 March 1883. He was buried in Highgate cemetery in London.

1848: revolution and the Communist Manifesto

Before looking in detail at the totality of Marx's writings on communism between 1844 and 1882, it is worth dwelling a little on the content of *The Manifesto of the Communist Party* (Marx and Engels, 1848). This remarkable little pamphlet provides us with a summary of a particular form of revolutionary communism, one which was to exert enormous influence over the communist movement (although its immediate impact was barely discernible). But it was not just a set of principles; it was also a political manifesto designed to create a particular type of political movement. It was thus a polemical piece, shaped in part by its desire to make a break with, or distinguish itself from the views of the utopian socialists, Icarian communists, Blanquists and others. In this way, we can see how Marx and Engels' ideas at times drew upon existing traditions and values, and at other times represented a distinct break from the ideas of their contemporaries.

The content of the *Manifesto* was the outcome of a series of pieces written in the latter half of 1847, including two pieces (written in the form of questions and answers) by Engels (Engels, 1847a and b). The *Communist Manifesto* was divided into four main sections. The opening section looked at the rise of the bourgeoisie. Section two examined the role of the communists in the coming revolution and of their relation to the proletariat as a whole. The third and fourth parts comprise an assortment of critiques and blasts at a variety of socialist thinkers and strands. Although it has become famous for some of its memorable lines ('the history of all hitherto existing society is the history of class struggles' or 'WORKING MEN OF ALL COUNTRIES, UNITE'), it also contains some crucial details on the nature of communism as a doctrine and a political movement. By setting out a range of communist principles – on topics like property, labour, education, the nation-state, the family – as well as the tactical and strategic mechanisms by which this society could be reached, Marx and Engels helped to focus the various strands of working-class protest and to define the meaning of communism in an industrial society. It was to become the first systematic depiction of the strategy, tactics, philosophy and world-view of communism in the modern era.

To the question, 'What is communism?', Engels gave the following answer: 'Communism is the doctrine of the conditions for the emancipation of the proletariat' (Engels, 1847a). The conditions for the emancipation of the proletariat meant the removal of those conditions exploiting and oppressing the workers, and the creation of those conditions that would liberate and emancipate the workers. The overall aim of the communists was to

organise society in such a way that every member of it can develop and use all his capabilities and powers in complete freedom and without thereby infringing the basic conditions of this society. (Engels, 1847b: 92)

Friedrich Engels

Engels was born in Barmen-Elberfeld in Germany on 28 November 1820. His father was a wealthy textile manufacturer. In 1838 Engels was sent to Bremen to work as a clerk by his father. It was not all study and work though: he drank a great deal, went regularly to the theatre and the opera and joined a choir and a fencing club.

Moving to Berlin in 1841 to complete his military service he was caught up in the atmosphere of intellectual radicalism of the Young Hegelians. In 1842 he went to Cologne where he met Moses Hess and Karl Marx. Hess convinced him that the communist revolution would take place first in England and so in 1843 he went to Manchester to work as a clerk in one of his father's textile factories. On witnessing the poverty and degradation of life there he wrote one of his most famous pamphlets, *The Condition of the Working Class in England in 1844*.

In August 1844 he met with Marx in Paris and the two realized that they shared the same views on capitalism. They began to work together publishing *The German Ideology* and the *Communist Manifesto*. Engels played an active part in the Revolutions of 1848, participating in an armed uprising against Prussian troops in Elberfeld, Baden and the Palatinate. When the revolt was defeated Engels escaped across the border to Switzerland and joined Marx in London.

Engels took a position in his father's factory in Manchester in 1850 and worked there for twenty years, not only to support himself, but also to support Marx to enable him to keep writing. The two kept in constant contact and they wrote to each other on average once every two days. Friedrich Engels sent postal orders of £1 or £5 notes, cut in half and sent in separate envelopes. In this way the Marx family was able to survive.

Engels moved to London in 1870, and continued to write and publish widely – on military affairs, natural science – as well as engaging in polemics with opponents of his 'Scientific Socialism'. After Marx's death in 1883, Engels devoted much of his time to editing and translating Marx's writings, and to work on feminism. He died, childless, of throat cancer on 5 August 1895.

Their immediate aim was to form the proletariat into a class, overthrow the supremacy of the bourgeoisie and have the proletariat seize political power. To clear away the conditions oppressing the workers, Marx and Engels posited the following as the distinguishing features of communism:

1 the abolition of private property;

2 the abolition of buying and selling (and the consequent disappearance of money);

3 the abolition of the division of labour;

4 the abolition of the personal appropriation of the products of labour;

5 the abolition of countries and nationality;

6 the abolition of the family.

These measures would remove the basis for the exploitation of the workers, and open the way for the emancipation and all-round development of the workers. The transition would be a gradual one, but would eventually result in a society where there would be:

- production run by society as a whole: for the good of society, according to a social plan;
- common use of all the instruments of production;
- common distribution of all products;
- labour as a means of enriching and promoting the life of the worker;
- communal education of children;
- openly legalized community of women.

How did they envisage the transition from the present to the communist future unfolding? This would take place in a number of stages, starting with the proletariat seizing political power from the bourgeoisie (and this would have to be a simultaneous revolution on an international scale, encompassing, according to Engels, Great Britain, USA, France and Germany), and leading to the seizure of all capital and the centralization of all elements of production in the hands of the state. This would necessarily mean 'despotic' measures (as the ruling class never gives up without a fight), and would vary from country to country. But, in the most advanced countries, Marx and Engels outlined that certain measures – for example creation of a national bank, state control of communications, transport and the means of production, abolition of child factory labour – would be necessary (Marx and Engels, 1848). The eventual outcome of this process would be a society whereby 'the free development of each is the condition for the free development of all' (Marx and Engels, 1848: 60).

In sum, a number of points stand out. First, the essential defining feature of communism was a negative one: the abolition of private property. This had enormous consequences for those who sought to realize Marx's vision, concentrating energies on the destruction of capitalism rather than on the creative act of making a communist society a reality. Secondly, the ultimate aim was a harmonious society of free, fully rounded, altruistic, sociable individuals. Thirdly, scarcity would be abolished: 'this development of industry will provide society with a sufficient quantity of products to satisfy the needs of all' (Engels, 1847a: 91). Fourthly, to achieve the society of material satisfaction and freedom required a transitional stage of political struggle, class conflict and despotic measures.

Marx and Engels on socialism and communism

The views contained in the writings of Marx and Engels for the creation of the manifesto of the Communist League in 1847 were not Marx and Engels' first speculations on this topic. Between 1844 and 1847, he wrote about the future society in *Private Property and Communism* in the *1844 Paris Manuscripts*, and *The German Ideology* (with Engels in 1845). After 1848, the views of Marx and Engels did not undergo any major reassessment (except when the experience of the Paris Commune suggested that the workers would have to destroy the state rather than just seize it and use it for their own ends). What we see after 1849 is greater detail and discussion of some of these points, but no major innovations or revisions. The main texts were *The Civil War in France* (1871), *The Critique of the Gotha Programme* (1875), along with sporadic references in *Grundrisse* and *Capital*.

The future society: an overview

The term 'communism' has a number of different meanings in Marx's writings. Marx used the term 'communism' in four ways:

– the stage that will succeed capitalism;

– the abolition of the private ownership of the means of production;

– the negation of the alienation, exploitation and oppression of the worker;

– a set of positive characteristics, including the emancipation of humanity, an increase in the productive forces in society, and the all-round development of the individual (de George, 1981).

Within Marx's view of communism there were both ethical components (emancipation, freedom, cooperation, etc.) and structural features of the future society. This cluster of ideas led to a number of different interpretations of Marxist communism emerging, as many variants could quite legitimately be identified from the different ways in which Marx described 'communism' in his writings. Marx and Engels also sketched in outline the manner in which the post-capitalist society progressively unfolded. The post-capitalist society contained three different stages (although the periodization was itself a little murky): the dictatorship of the proletariat, socialism (the 'lower' phase of communism) and full communism (the 'higher' phase). The dictatorship of the proletariat was the regime which would rule in the period after the proletarian revolution. But what did Marx (and Engels) mean by this term? How long would it last?

In the *Critique of the Gotha Programme*, Marx identified the 'lower' phase of communism (later termed 'socialism' by Engels) as a prolonged historical period in which capitalist society would be negated, as the foundations of capitalist exploitation were removed (Marx and Engels, 1875). This however was a transitional phase. The negation of the features of capitalist society would gradually evolve into the positive features of communist society, as socialism was transformed into full communism. Under this 'higher' phase, the individual becomes the conscious master of nature, and of his/her destiny.

The future society: the 'lower' phase

The lower phase was marked by elements of continuity with capitalism: classes, the division of labour, wage labour and elements of inequality would still exist as remuneration would be carried out 'according to work done'. But the process of transformation gets under way simultaneously, as the exploitative features of capitalism – the market, private property – are negated and replaced by structures which promote a communist society. These include:

- the abolition of private property and its replacement with public ownership;
- the means of production brought under central direction and control;
- measures adopted to foment the most rapid possible development of the productive forces (which include the means of production, the labour process, technological innovations and so on) (Marx and Engels, 1848: 52–53).

The politics of the transition period were slightly more complex. For Marx the state under all previous societies was an organ of class rule. It was used by the ruling class in any epoch to oppress other classes and realize its own interests. It did this by posing its own particular interests as the embodiment of the interests of society as a whole. One of the primary tasks of the socialist revolution was to destroy the basis of political exploitation, and thereby create the opportunity to build a society without a state. How did Marx envisage moving from the coercive state apparatus under capitalism to a non-class, non-state society? Marx's views on the post-revolutionary state were guarded, except in his writings on the Paris Commune in *The Civil War in France*, and ambiguous. At one point Marx talks about the need to smash the state and move immediately to a form of administration based on the Paris Commune: 'the working class cannot simply lay hold of the ready-made state machinery and wield it for its own purposes' (Marx and Engels, 1871: 285). At other points (and Marx is noticeably silent on the Paris Commune after 1871) it is necessary during the transition to the 'higher phase' that the proletariat are able to wield power through a coercive organism: the dictatorship of the proletariat. Its function is to oppress the bourgeois classes, and appropriate the means of production for the common good. This entailed taking over and utilizing the existing state machinery. This was a transitional state, however. As progress towards the higher phase unfolded, the need for a coercive state would disappear.

The meaning of the dictatorship of the proletariat in Marx's writings is very unclear. How long would the dictatorship of the proletariat last? What form of democracy did Marx envisage? How would the proletariat control the state? How would the state enforce its rule over the non-proletarian classes? How would the proletariat undertake the transformation of the economy? How would the proletarian dictatorship be transformed into the stateless society of the 'higher' phase of communism? Would it be abolished by the proletariat, as envisaged by Marx? Or would it 'wither away', as envisaged by Engels? All of these questions remained frustratingly undeveloped in Marx's writings, although this has not stopped scholars from speculating at length!

The future society: the 'higher phase'

The unfolding of the historical process would lead inexorably from the lower to the higher phase of communist society. In a vivid passage, Marx describes how in a communist society it will be organized on the basis of 'from each according to his ability, to each according to his needs' (Marx and Engels, 1871: 320–21).

Communism meant the full and final self-realization of the individual: people were now in full control of their own destiny. The abolition of market forces promoted conscious rational control over the economy. All sources of alienation and inequality have been abolished: the social division of labour, classes, wage-labour, production for exchange-value and the coercive apparatus of the state. All the divisive dichotomies of capitalist society – mental/manual labour, town/country, male/female – would be overcome.

In economic terms, production is directed towards use-value, not profit. Ownership of the means of production is completely socialized. Developments in technology and labour productivity enable the production of a superabundance of goods. This entailed the abolition of scarcity, which was to become a central goal of the Bolsheviks after 1917. Under communism there is also a totally different approach to work. Individuals contribute according to their abilities, and draw from the common supply of goods to meet their needs. In his earlier writings Marx suggests that labour will be fulfilling, diverse and creative. The abolition of the social division of labour would be replaced by a voluntary division of labour:

. . . while in communist society, where nobody has one exclusive sphere of activity but each can become accomplished in any branch he wishes, society regulates the general production and thus makes it possible for me to do one thing today and another tomorrow, to hunt in the morning, fish in the afternoon, rear cattle in the evening, criticise after dinner, just as I have a mind, without ever becoming hunter, fisherman, cowherd or critic. (Marx, 1845: 169)

In his later works, labour has a slightly different status. Marx sets labour entirely within the 'realm of necessity' (the production of requirements necessary for biological survival). The time spent on work of this kind is greatly reduced by the growth in the productive forces, and by a voluntary division of labour arising from a process of education. This creates the preconditions for the 'realm of freedom', when individuals are able to develop their potential to their full ability, *in their leisure time* (Walicki, 1995: 86–7). According to Marx in *Capital* 'the sphere of material production remains a realm of necessity, and the true realm of freedom begins only in leisure time' (Marx, 1867: 512). In other words, people exercise their creativity and realize themselves not in work, but outside work. Politics no longer exists under communism. The destruction of the division of labour and of a class-based society removes the basis for a coercive state apparatus which will disappear eventually. In its stead there would be a non-political authority, or administration of communist society which is communitarian, democratic, participative and non-coercive.

Marx on socialism and communism – a summary

The dominant themes of Marx's writings on socialism and communism were shaped by his world-view which synthesized various intellectual currents of the nineteenth century: rationalism, materialism, optimism. Marx had an optimistic view of humanity. Freed from the fetters and constraints of bourgeois society, individuals could live harmoniously with one another. Removing the basis for exploitation, and overcoming alienation would facilitate the emergence of a society of harmony, unity and voluntary cooperation. Human beings were essentially social beings, who discovered their true humanity in a social context. But Marx also saw production and the growth of productive power as the key to unlocking this harmonious society. Developments in technology and production would enable scarcity to be abolished, and this was the crucial factor enabling the strife and exploitation of capitalism to be transcended. The final outcome of history was a society free from alienation, in which the individual realizes him- or herself fully, and becomes truly human for the first time.

The debates about the nature of the communist society envisaged by Marx and Engels, and the meaning of many of these unresolved issues died down after the 1870s. The energy and focus of socialist and communist parties and activists were channelled instead into paving the way for either reforms to capitalism to create a socialist system, or for the revolution that would overthrow capitalism and the rule of the bourgeoisie and inaugurate a proletarian state dedicated to the construction of a communist system. Marx had played a key role in this process before his death in 1883. Marx was not just an abstract thinker. He was also committed to political activism, to changing the world, to influencing the course of development of the workers movement. Modern communism was not just a set of ideas. It also gave birth to a political movement, organized along international lines. After 1848, the moves to create a workers movement transcending national boundaries, to advance the interests of the proletariat, began to gather pace. The spectre was assuming a collective form and beginning to organize itself to take on its oppressors.

The evolution of the communist movement 1850–1915

The year 1848 was a key moment for the communist movement. The failure of the revolutions in France, Germany, Austro-Hungary, Sicily, Naples, Lombardy, Venice and Rome was complete by the end of 1849/50. The failure of Cabet's communitarian movement in the USA spelt the demise of the attempt to create an alternative civilization within the confines of the existing system (with the exception of a variety of millenarian religious movements). What lessons did Marx and Engels draw from the events of 1848/49? Their position when the revolutions broke out was that the bourgeoisie, aided and abetted by the petit-bourgeoisie and the workers, would overturn the rule of European autocracies and the aristocracy. This would then lead quickly to a conflict between the workers and the bourgeoisie culminating in a second revolution. But the workers had been let down by the 'traitorous' bourgeoisie. In their Address of the Central Committee to the Communist League in March 1850, Marx and Engels asserted three things. First, that the workers' party must have the maximum degree of organization, unity and independence, to prevent its being betrayed by the bourgeoisie in the future. Secondly, Marx reiterated their aim was not 'simply to modify private property, but to abolish it, not to hush up class antagonisms but to abolish classes, not to improve the existing society, but to found a new one' (Marx and Engels, 1850). Marx emphasized what distinguished the communists from the anarchists, and the socialists: revolutionary, not reformist; internationalist, not nationalist; class warriors, not class conciliators; abolishers not mitigators of private property; centralists, not localists. Thirdly, Marx and Engels called for 'permanent revolution', for an independently organized political party of the proletariat. It was to this end that attention was diverted after 1850.

The First International: 1864–73

The defeat of 1848 made the Communist League a banned organization in France and Germany, and it moved its headquarters to London. Disputes among the leadership led to its effective demise. Marx moved the headquarters to Cologne, and the long work of preparing the workers for the conflict with the bourgeoisie was driven underground (Cole, 1958; Lichtheim, 1975). It was not until 1862 that moves to revive an international workers movement began to gather pace. The origins of the first International Working Men's Association is a complex one, involving the confluence of a number of different strands – trade unionism, workers' solidarity, anti-slavery, factory reform, democratic republicanism – in a number of different countries (Great Britain, Germany, France, Italy, Poland). In November 1864 these came together when Marx was invited to deliver an inaugural address, which was adopted as its statement of aims by the Geneva Congress in 1865. Marx highlighted two import-ant features of the period between 1848 and 1863. First, the passage of factory reform acts demonstrated that if the workers organized themselves they could prevail in a struggle against the bourgeoisie. Secondly, the cooperative factory movement of the Owenites had demonstrated that production on a large scale could be carried out without a class of exploiters in charge, and that hired wage labour was destined to die out. However, he went on to state that

. . . *the experience of the period 1848–64 has proved beyond doubt that, however excellent in principle and however useful in practice, co-operative labour . . . will never be able to arrest the growth in geometrical progression of monopoly, to free the masses, nor even to perceptibly lighten the burden of their miseries.* (Marx, 1864)

The solution? To develop international proletarian solidarity and cooperative labour, the conquest of political power by the workers had to be achieved. This was the overriding goal of the labour movement. But should this be via a violent revolution? Or could it be achieved by peaceful means via the ballot box?

The demise of the IWMA came in the aftermath of the abortive Paris Commune in 1871. In March of that year, Parisian workers revolted and the uprising was not finally suppressed until 28 May 1871. The presence of many of the leaders of the

IWMA in the uprising led many moderates to leave the organization. After a great deal of dissension and disagreement, Marx moved the headquarters to the USA where it finally disappeared from view in 1876. The failure of the Paris uprising seemed to Marx to mark the end of the revolutionary ideals that he had worked for (Kolakowski, 1978).

It wasn't until 1889 that the workers movement managed to regroup. On 14 July two broad groupings (a 'Marxist' one and a 'non-Marxist' one) agreed to join together, primarily to unite the French and German workers and so prevent a European conflict. It formally adopted the basic principles outlined by Marx in his earlier works – class struggle, international unity, proletarian action and the socialization of the means of production – but in practice these ideas were open to a variety of interpretations, and so the Second International became an exceptionally broad church. There were two persistent fault-lines running through it: the tension between the reformist and revolutionary wings, and that between the national and international advocates. The reformist strand grew much stronger across this period, especially in the areas where liberal democracy was becoming more established, as opportunities for electoral power and improvements to the lot of the workers through legislative means seemed to grow. The growth of 'revisionism' (a movement advanced by Eduard Bernstein, arguing the need to revise or update Marxism in the light of the changes to capitalism) seemed to herald the victory of reformism in the European labour movement. The victory of the nationalists over the internationalists seemed to be confirmed in 1914 when most socialists lined up behind their nation-states in the dreadful conflict of the First World War. The year 1914 marked the great divide in the workers movement between the reformist socialists and social democrats on the one hand, and the communists and revolutionaries on the other (Sassoon, 1997).

The revolutionary, internationalist flame was not totally extinguished though. The radical wing, which led in 1917 to the victory of the communists in Russia, continued where the labour movement was confronted with authoritarian regimes, most notably in Russia. But it also maintained a presence in Western and Central Europe through the continued existence of radical voices and wings of ostensibly reformist movements. For example, the SPD (Social Democratic Party in Germany) contained a radical grouping, centred on Karl Liebknecht and Rosa Luxemburg who were committed to revolution, and were to form the core of the German Communist Party in 1918. The centre of gravity of the communist movement shifted eastwards however and settled around the Russian Social Democratic Labour Party (RSDLP), which was founded in 1898. Communism in the twentieth century cannot be understood without reference to the country and the party where it first came to power.

Marxism and communism in Russia: 1898–1917

The acknowledged founder of the Marxist movement in Russia was Georgi Plekhanov (Kolakowski, 1978). In 1883, he, along with Vera Zasulich and Pavel Axelrod, created the Emancipation of Labour Group in Geneva. In 1898, the RSDLP was formed in Minsk. The autocratic context of revolutionary politics meant that the party had to operate in a clandestine, conspiratorial manner. A tightly knit, relatively small organization would be much more difficult to infiltrate, but also ran the risk of being an elitist, minority movement, detached from the masses. At the outset, it was marked by a high degree of internal conflict over specific components of revolutionary strategy, while sharing a set of common assumptions about the future of the post-revolutionary society. The key figure in the development of a Russian brand of Marxism, and for the subsequent history of communism in the USSR and beyond, was Lenin.

Vladimir Ilych Ulyanov (Lenin)

Lenin was born on 10 (22) April 1870. His father was inspector of schools in the region of Simbirsk, while his mother was the daughter of a land-owning physician. His early life was marred by two tragedies: the death of his father from a cerebral haemorrhage in 1886 and the execution of his brother Alexander for his part in the plot to assassinate Alexander III. The death of his brother was the spur that drove Lenin to become the ruthless revolutionary activist who was to overturn the history of Russia.

Lenin went to university in Kazan. He got involved in revolutionary movements and his outlook was profoundly affected by two books: the novel *What is to be done?* by Nikolai Chernyshevsky, and Marx's *Das Kapital*. He was soon expelled from Kazan University. His mother moved the family to Samara and he lived and worked there for a couple of years before moving to St Petersburg in 1893.

He was arrested in December 1895 and exiled to Shushenskoye in Siberia. At some point he changed his name to Lenin as his revolutionary pseudonym. No one is exactly sure why he chose Lenin, although it is thought that it was a version of the river Lena. In July 1898 he married Nadezhda Krupskaya. In 1899 he published his first major work, *The Development of Capitalism in Russia*.

When his exile ended he travelled extensively in Europe, moving to Zurich, Geneva, Munich, Prague, Vienna and London. He headed up the Bolshevik faction of the RSDLP after it split in

1903. A dedicated opponent of the First World War, Lenin was taken aback by the overthrow of the autocracy in February 1917 and had to rely on the Imperial German government to get back to Russia. Once there he transformed the Bolsheviks into the main opposition grouping to the Provisional Government and orchestrated the October Revolution.

Lenin oversaw the victory in the Civil War, and the first steps in the construction of the Soviet state. Although he survived an assassination attempt in August 1918, a bullet remained lodged in his neck. His health deteriorated rapidly after 1922. In May 1922 he had his first stroke. A second soon followed in December 1922, and a third in March 1923 left him bedridden and unable to speak. Lenin died on 21 January 1924. After his death the city of Petrograd was renamed Leningrad. His body was preserved and put on permanent display in the Lenin mausoleum in Red Square on 27 January 1924.

Lenin played a formative role in creating a type of revolutionary movement which was to be adopted across the world in the period after 1917 as a vehicle for communist parties attempting to seize power. This organizational pattern also became a blueprint for government once communist parties came to power. Lenin's approach emphasized three things. First, Lenin was uncompromisingly revolutionary rather than reformist in his approach. Nothing should ever stand in the way of the revolution. All actions were judged against a single criterion: did it advance the revolutionary cause or not? Lenin's world-view was ruthlessly amoral. Any means justified the revolutionary end. Secondly, Lenin devised a model of the appropriate structure for a revolutionary party, a model which was shaped by his views on revolutionary consciousness and by the Russian context. Thirdly, Lenin was uncompromisingly and fiercely internationalist in his outlook. He was deeply committed to the international revolution and to international proletarian solidarity.

The debates over party structure and revolutionary strategy were bitter ones indeed. Right from its birth, the RSDLP contained many factions. Just five years later, these factions resulted in the division of the RSDLP into two wings in 1903. The issue was one of party organization. Divisions emerged over whether the party should be an elite vanguard of professional revolutionaries, or a mass movement. Lenin argued (in line with Plekhanov's earlier works) in *What is to be Done?* that the workers by themselves could only attain to 'trade-union consciousness', that is, a concern with their immediate material needs (wages, conditions, etc.). To attain to 'Social Democrat' (that is, revolutionary) consciousness required a disciplined organization of revolutionaries, armed with the 'correct' ideology, who would lead and guide the workers:

Hence our task, the task of Social-Democracy, is to combat spontaneity, to divert the working class movement from this spontaneous trade-unionist striving to come under the wing of the bourgeoisie, and to bring it under the wing of revolutionary Social-Democracy. (Lenin, 1902: 40)

Clearly, there was an important practical aspect to this theory. A mass movement was inappropriate in the repressive conditions of Tsarism. The context of Lenin's writings is also vital. The pamphlet was part of the wider polemical struggle with the 'Economists' (a group who favoured concentrating their energies on the workers' struggle for better conditions in the factory). Although Lenin always stressed the importance of mass action, his conception of the revolutionary party was based upon the need for a dedicated revolutionary elite, armed with the correct ideology, who would lead the masses to revolution and guide the subsequent process of international revolution and the construction of a global communist system. Yet the stress on the need for a dedicated revolutionary elite separate from the mass movement caused a split at the 1903 Congress, where Lenin and Martov fell out over the definition of party membership (Service, 1985). Lenin prevailed at the Congress and subsequently became the dominant figure in Russian Marxism. The resulting division (Bolsheviks and Mensheviks) created two wings of the RSDLP until 1912 when the split became final and irrevocable.

It was the Bolshevik (majority) grouping, led by Lenin, which was the most vocal in its criticisms of those European socialists who supported their governments in the First World War. Committed to the doctrine of proletarian internationalism, the Bolsheviks remained deeply opposed to the conflict, and urged all workers and workers' parties to oppose the conflict and to work for a democratic peace. The Bolsheviks were critical of European socialists who appeared to have taken the line of reformism and nationalism rather than revolution and internationalism. In 1915, Lenin published a significant pamphlet, *Imperialism: the Highest Stage of Capitalism*. Lenin argued that the nature of capitalism had undergone a profound transformation. They were now living in an era of Imperial monopoly capitalism. The internationalization of capitalism had created a situation where all the capitalist economies were interlinked and interdependent. Lenin was quick to see the revolutionary implications of this. He argued that, as the capitalist countries were now interdependent, the international proletarian revolution might break out in the 'weakest link' in the Imperial chain (i.e. Russia) rather than the most advanced capitalist countries (i.e. Great

Britain or Germany) as argued by Marx. The overthrow of capitalism in Russia would provoke, domino-like, a series of revolutions across Europe. The outcome? Global revolution. Revolution in Russia was now on the agenda.

Although Lenin had changed the sequence of the outbreak of revolution, and had established a central role for the party in the revolution itself, he remained committed to Marx's key principles of a communist movement: international unity, class struggle, socialization of the means of production and egalitarianism. They sought to eradicate all forms of discrimination and injustice: gender, nationality and class. All Russian Marxists maintained their allegiance and loyalty to Marx's vision of communism. What was unclear in the period before 1917 was how they would get to this state from where they were: war-torn, socially divided, economically underdeveloped Russia. This transitional phase – otherwise known as socialism – raised critical questions. Should the capitalist state be captured or smashed? How, and by whom should political power be exercised? How would the economy be organized on the road to communism? How could international revolution be carried out in Europe? All these questions had to be resolved after October 1917, alongside the small task of retaining power and winning a civil war. The acquisition of power in October 1917 brought the Bolsheviks a world to transform. The Bolsheviks were about to take their first steps in the realization of their vision: to make the whole world communist.

Conclusion: communism before power

Does 'modern' communism have anything in common with the earlier form of communism? Clearly, lines of continuity can be traced between the two. The commitment to radical egalitarianism, and the desire to build social and economic structures and organizations which promoted communalism were both reproduced in the communism which emerged in the nineteenth century amid the flux of industrialization, urbanization and the rise of the proletariat. But these elements of continuity look very different if we scratch beneath the surface and examine the context, rationale and the meaning of these terms. The egalitarianism and communalism of 'early' communism was derived from an aspiration to alleviate the suffering of the poor and oppressed. Although 'modern' communism was concerned with the suffering of the masses, its aim was to emancipate the masses, not to alleviate their suffering. The communal experiments of early communism were essentially agrarian, whereas the 'modern' communist movement was an urban movement, concerned with redressing the unequal distribution of power and wealth between the proletariat and the bourgeoisie.

But 'modern' communism also marked a break with the earlier ideals at a deeper level, in terms of scope, means and aims. 'Modern' communism sought to replace the existing society rather than to create alternative communities living counter-culturally as examples of a different type of society. Modern communism became, especially after the Babouvists, an organized political movement striving to effect change rather than theoretical speculations or fantastical dreamings from the imaginations of thinkers or philosophers. Although this continued through the writings and example of Cabet, Fourier, Owen et al., these all died down by the mid nineteenth century and communism became a movement for the emancipation of the workers. 'Modern' communism, because of industrialization and the rise of the nation-state and imperialism, became an international movement rather than an eclectic collection of local expressions, punctuating the historical stage sporadically. Modern communism ceased to be derived from an essentially religious world-view, and instead became a secularized political movement. Modern communism, as specified by Marx, looked to create a new society in the future rather than looking backwards to restore a 'lost' golden age. In sum, modern communism was a movement which sought to overthrow capitalism and create the conditions for the emancipation of all peoples from the various forms of oppression that assailed them, and so create a world of harmony, cooperation and equality.

Recommended reading

For good background to this period, see E. Hobsbawm, *The Age of Revolution* (Weidenfeld & Nicolson, 1992). Details on the growth of socialism can be found in G. Lichtheim, *A Short History of Socialism* (Fontana, 1975); G.D.H. Cole, *A History of Socialist Thought* (Macmillan, 1958); L. Kolakowski, *Main Currents of Marxism* (Clarendon Press, 1978). For the works of the utopian socialists, see K. Taylor, *The Political Ideas of the Utopian Socialists* (Frank Cass, 1982); C. Johnson, *Utopian Communism in France: Etienne Cabet and the Icarians* (Cornell University Press, 1974).

On Marx and Marxism, then, you will need to read the key texts of Marx and Engels, *The German Ideology* (1845); *The Manifesto of the Communist Party* (1848); *Capital* (1867); *The Civil War in France* (1871); *Socialism: Utopian and Scientific* (1892). All can be found in *Collected Works* (Lawrence & Wishart, 1974 onwards). Commentaries on Marx's view of communism can be found in A. Walicki, *Marxism and the Leap to the Kingdom of Freedom: The Rise and Fall of the Communist Utopia* (Stanford University Press, 1995); J.P. Burke, L. Crocker and L. Legters, *Marxism and the Good Society* (Cambridge University Press, 1981); W. Laqueur and L. Labedz (eds), *The Future of Communist Society* (Praeger, 1962).

For works on socialism and communism up to 1917, see D. Sassoon, *One Hundred Years of Socialism: The West European Left in the Twentieth Century* (Fontana, 1997); N. Harding, *Lenin's Political Thought vols 1 and 2* (Macmillan, 1981); D. McLellan, *Marxism After Marx* (Macmillan, 1979); J. Plamenatz, *German Marxism and Russian Communism* (Longman, 1954).

CHAPTER 3

Communism in the USSR: The early years 1917–53

Introduction

COMMUNISM IN THE twentieth century was dominated by the Soviet experience. Arising out of the chaos in Russia at the end of the First World War, the Bolshevik Party came to power intent on constructing Marx's vision of communism. The pattern of socio-economic development and political power established in the USSR became a template that was exported to Eastern Europe, Asia and Africa across the twentieth century, forming a bloc of communist states. In the period between 1929 and 1956, it appeared that communism as a movement would eclipse capitalism and become the dominant global social system. How did communism come to be synonymous with the Soviet experience?

The victory of Bolshevism in Russia created the world's first state dedicated to the construction of communism. Although non-Soviet communist movements continued to exist, increasingly communism and the Soviet experience became closely tied together. As the Bolsheviks consolidated their power, they began to theorize the nature of the communist society in more detail; they began to work out how to achieve this in practice and also how this might be exported abroad. In this way, the USSR spelt out a particular interpretation of the theory and practice of Marxian communism. This is not to say that this was an authentic variant of Marxian communism, but merely that it was the Bolshevik interpretation of communism. The Bolshevik model of building a communist society has caused communism in popular consciousness to be identified with the Soviet experience.

How did communism become synonymous with the USSR and Comintern?

The position of the USSR as the fulcrum of the communist movement came about as a result of a series of events between 1914 and 1923. The split in the socialist movement caused by the onset of world war between the reformist, nationally oriented parties on the one hand, and the revolutionary, international parties on the other, left just a few groups to carry the communist torch, most notable of which were the Bolsheviks in Russia and the Spartacists in Germany. The Bolsheviks came to power in Russia in October 1917, but they expected there to be a European-wide socialist revolution to follow on. However, in Germany in 1918, in Italy in 1919 and in Hungary in 1920, communist revolts and uprisings were brutally crushed. This left the Bolsheviks as the only revolutionary party still in power after the chaos of the First World War had died down. They now had to confront the

monumental task of holding on to power and building communism in Russia, while attempting to instigate revolution abroad.
What were the implications for communist theory and practice
of the fact that it was Lenin and his Bolshevik Party that came to
power, and that it was successful in one country only?

First, the Bolsheviks were committed to implementing Marx's
vision. This entailed a number of 'negative' actions – abolishing
private property, buying and selling, the division of labour – as
well as more 'positive' actions – socializing the means of production – to be implemented. However, there was also a great deal
of vagueness about what these things actually meant in detail. So
the Bolsheviks had to work out what this meant in practice.

Secondly, the Bolsheviks had to balance short-term imperatives with their longer-term vision. In particular they had to
balance two sets of imperatives. First, they had to maintain
themselves in power in the face of various forms and intensities
of opposition: international capitalist hostility (mainly military
and diplomatic); internal class opposition (from the old classes
who had been dispossessed by the October Revolution); popular
resentment at unpopular policies (most notably from the peasants, but also from non-Russian nationalities and some elements
of the working class); and finally political antipathy from other
socialist groups in Russia who had been marginalized after October.
The second set of imperatives revolved around the modernization of Russia – economically, culturally, socially – in order to
build the foundations necessary for communism, which required
a technologically advanced industrial economy and a culturally
sophisticated literate population able to undertake many tasks,
including participation in the running of the country. But this
posed a dilemma. What if modernization required measures

diametrically opposed to their long-term vision? What if a rigid division of labour, private property, the market (i.e. capitalist practices) all proved to be the most efficient method of modernizing Russia?

Thirdly, the Bolsheviks were ardent internationalists, but the expected international revolution had not materialized. This meant that the Bolsheviks had to 'go it alone' initially, while at the same time working out how to create an international movement for proletarian revolution. But which should take priority?

Finally, the Soviet version of communism was stamped with the influence of Bolshevik thinking and practice. In particular, the Bolshevik mentality – uncompromising, ruthless, militant, amoral – imbued Soviet style communism with a steely determination to focus on the ends and not the means. Anything could be justified as long as it fulfilled one simple criterion: did it assist the state in its attempts to build socialism and communism? Bolshevik political practice, especially in terms of the role of the party, was also marked by a high degree of elitism, centralization and hierarchy. Consequently, the post-revolutionary political system was likely to be highly centralized, with the party at the heart of everything. These factors were profoundly important in giving a precise shape, colour and texture to communism Soviet-style.

The Bolshevik understanding of communism

Although the Bolsheviks were almost immediately pitched into a bitter and destructive civil war, they never lost sight of the importance of theory in their project to build communism. As a political group with a clear aim in mind, it was essential that the political leadership were able to align their present policies with their long-term goals. Spelling out the details of the communist society, as well as the means to get there, was crucial to ensure that they were moving in the right direction. But there was also a political dimension to this. It was a matter of political legitimacy for the Bolshevik Party to be able to show that the USSR was moving towards communism. Unless this could be demonstrated in practice, it would call into question their claims about the future. This in turn required details of what Soviet society would look like as it approached communism. This accounts for the seemingly puzzling amount of time and energy that the Bolsheviks devoted to questions of theory and the future, in the midst of a life-and-death struggle for survival, economic collapse, infrastructural decay and bitter criticism from socialists inside and outside Russia.

The key document produced by the Bolsheviks (who renamed themselves the Russian Communist Party [Bolsheviks] in 1919) after 1917 was the party programme of 1919 (Bukharin & Preobrazhensky, 1969). The party programme set out the long-term perspectives of the party alongside a collection of short-term policy commitments. The first programme had been introduced in 1903, but the party leadership decided at the 8th Party Congress in March 1919 that the time was right to update the programme in the light of all that had happened since 1903. A new party programme was discussed and adopted. It was accompanied by a pamphlet – the *ABC of Communism* written by Nikolai Bukharin and Evgenii Preobrazhensky – which was designed to popularize and explain the programme to the masses, and thus help the people to understand what the Bolsheviks stood for, what they were trying to achieve and what communism would mean.

The party programme did not say much about the ultimate future society. This was spelt out in the *ABC*. The party programme focused instead on how to build the road to communism. How was the future communist society described in the *ABC*? In a communist society, the means of production and exchange are owned by society, organized according to a plan, and have put an end to exploitation and class divisions. Communist society puts an end to the division of labour and frees people to fulfil their potential:

Under communism, for example, there will not be permanent managers of factories, nor will there be persons who do one and the same kind of work throughout their lives. Under capitalism, if a man is a boot-maker, he spends his whole life in making boots . . . Nothing of this sort happens in communist society. Under communism people receive a many-sided culture, and find themselves at home in various branches of production: today I work in an administrative capacity, I reckon up how many felt boots or how many French rolls must be produced in the following month; tomorrow I shall be working in a soap factory, next month perhaps in a steam-laundry, and the month after in an electric power station. This will be possible when all the members of society have been suitably educated. (Bukharin and Preobrazhensky, 1969: 115–116)

How are goods distributed under communism? As there will be an abundance of goods, they will be supplied according to the needs of the people. How will this be organized?

. . . products are not exchanged one for another; they are neither bought nor sold. They are simply stored in the communal warehouses, and are subsequently delivered to those who need them. In such conditions, money will no longer be required. A person will take from the communal

storehouse precisely as much as he needs, no more. No one will have any interest in taking more than he wants in order to sell the surplus to others, since all these others can satisfy their needs whenever they please. (Bukharin and Preobrazhensky, 1969: 116)

There will be no politics under communism, merely an administration to ensure that everything runs smoothly. A workers state will be required for two to three generations in order to oversee the expropriation of the old classes and the elimination of hostility, laziness and criminality. Eventually this will die out and

[t]here will be no need for special ministers of State, for police and prisons, for laws and decrees – nothing of the sort. Just as in an orchestra all the performers watch the conductor's baton and act accordingly, so here all will consult the statistical reports and will direct their work accordingly. The State, therefore, has ceased to exist. (Bukharin and Preobrazhensky, 1969: 118)

What then were the advantages of communism? First, it would eliminate the waste of human and material resources currently absorbed by wars, the free market, politics and class struggle. Secondly, it would accelerate technological development. Thirdly, it would remove the 'parasites' who contribute nothing to the welfare of society. Fourthly, workers would no longer have to work as long, or as hard: 'The working day will grow continually shorter, and people will be to an increasing extent freed from the chains imposed on them by nature' (Bukharin and Preobrazhensky, 1969: 121).

In order to reach communism, the *ABC* spelt out a central role for the Communist Party. As the most advanced, organized expression of communist consciousness, the party would lead the struggle for the interests of the proletariat, which would inevitably mean crushing opposition, putting down resistance, and generally being ruthless,

In extreme cases, the workers government must not hesitate to use the method of terror. Only when the suppression of the exploiters is complete, when they have ceased to resist, when it is no longer in their power to injure the working class, will the proletarian dictatorship grow progressively milder. (Bukharin and Preobrazhensky, 1969: 125)

Herein lay one of the paradoxes of communism Soviet-style. The end point was a noble vision of a society of liberation, cooperation, harmony, material abundance, rule by the people, fulfilling work and ample leisure time. The road to get there was one of ruthless expropriation, dictatorial government, maximum economic centralization and efficiency, and compulsory labour. Can freedom be reached through profoundly illiberal, often 'terroristic' paths? What would this road look like in practice?

The 1919 Party Programme contained sections dealing with politics, nationality, religion, military affairs, justice, education, the economy, agriculture, distribution, money and banking, finance, housing, social welfare and public hygiene. The focus of the programme was not so much about defining and specifying the final communist society, but was concerned more with the transitional phase. The task here was to construct the foundations of communism, which meant a period of demolition and removing the rubble of capitalism and autocracy in Russia, before pressing ahead with the building project. This entailed measures to remove the structures and conditions which produced exploitation and oppression, and also measures to liberate and empower the masses.

In terms of politics, the programme outlined the need to replace bourgeois democracy with proletarian democracy, to ensure the maximum possible participation by the masses in the process of governing. This meant abolishing the old forms of local and central government and judicial organization, and the creation of new political structures which put power in the hands of the masses. The programme did recognize a number of problems that were created by the Russian context. First, the low educational levels of the population. This necessitated a good deal of work on the part of the party to increase the cultural and educational levels of the population to enable them to govern the country. Secondly, the possibility of counter-revolution. The Bolsheviks recognized in the short term the need to impose restrictions on the political rights of the 'old' classes, in order to ensure that they did not regain power and reimpose the old exploitative system of class domination. In time though, these restrictions would die out. Thirdly, the lack of experience in governing. In order to fulfil Marx's vision of a stateless society, this required a system whereby all would take their turn at participating in the administration of the country. This was a long-term aim. In the meantime, however, the country had to be governed, and this required using people who had experience: in some cases this meant members of the old classes. Overall then, the programme stood directly in line with Marx's vision of a democratic stateless society run by and for the proletariat. However, the interim period was likely to see an enhanced role for the party, and a strongly authoritarian approach to remove the powers and rights of the old classes.

In terms of the economy, the programme highlighted the need to continue the expropriation of the bourgeoisie and to hasten the maximum possible centralization and concentration of the economy to ensure that industry and agriculture got back to work as quickly as possible. The trade unions had a vital role to play in cooperating with the state to ensure that the workers participated fully in the reconstruction process itself. But the party also recognized the need to use the old experts and in the short term to reward them disproportionately, notwithstanding their long-term commitment to introduce radical equality. Banks would be run by the state, but money would not disappear immediately. However, the state would take measures to create the conditions for the abolition of money in the future. Finally, the programme also highlighted the importance of the large-scale socialization of agriculture, to increase production and to create a rural proletariat in the Russian countryside.

Socially, the programme set out an ambitious agenda for the emancipation of women, for an extensive scheme of social welfare, public hygiene and public health, for measures to control and eradicate religion, and also an all-embracing educational programme. Given the importance of upgrading the cultural and educational levels of the population, this 11-point schema was not only vital to provide the people with a technical and cultural education to enable them to work in an advanced economy and to participate in the administration of society, but it was also a crucial mechanism by which the party hoped to instil a communist consciousness in the people (Bukharin and Preobrazhensky, 1969: 444–45).

With regard to the international arena, the programme argued that, in an era of imperialist wars and national civil wars, there was no place for pacifism or faith in international tribunals. Only an international proletarian revolution would put an end to imperialism, war, conflict and strife. To achieve this required an irrevocable break with the socialist and social-democratic parties of Western Europe who had sided with the bourgeoisie during the First World War. The vehicle for promoting the international revolution would be a new body: the Third Communist International, headed by the RCP.

This party programme attempted to synthesize the communist vision set out by Marx with the problematic reality of Russia in 1919. How did the Bolsheviks set about trying to build communism in these four areas: politics, the economy, society and internationally?

Exporting communism: Comintern and the Third International

Lenin and the other Bolshevik leaders had expected the revolution overthrowing the bourgeoisie to be an international one. The international dimension was seen as crucial if the revolution was to survive (a proletarian government would undoubtedly face armed opposition from the imperial powers) but also if communism was to be built. The low level of Russian economic and cultural development meant that the Russian workers would require material assistance and expert help from the workers of the more advanced countries. The full victory of the revolution in one country was deemed to be impossible without outside assistance. However, by the end of the First World War, it was becoming clear that the likelihood of an imminent international revolution was receding fast.

All Bolsheviks continued to insist on the importance of the international revolution, *in the long run*. But this imperative had to be balanced against the need to ensure that the Soviet state survived, as a beacon of hope for workers everywhere. How did the Bolsheviks go about achieving this? On seizing power in October 1917, the party was faced with the imminent problem of the First World War. Lenin, Stalin, Litvinov and others argued that the Bolsheviks should make peace with Germany to ensure the survival of the revolution. Trotsky, Bukharin and others argued that the war should continue, and be turned into a revolutionary war: export revolution abroad by force of arms. The failure of the German workers to rise up convinced Lenin to sign a humiliating peace treaty at Brest-Litovsk on 3 March 1918, in which Russia lost a third of its population, 32% of its cultivable land, 27% of its railways, 54% of its industry and 89% of its coal mines. Although the leadership were deeply criticized by the ardent revolutionaries and internationalists, the Treaty of Brest-Litovsk gave them a slight 'breathing-space' to reorder their priorities (Carr, 1966, vol. 2 and vol. 3). In the summer of 1918, a destructive civil war broke out between the communists and their supporters on the one hand, and the Whites (the old classes) and the allied capitalist powers on the other. Russia was subject to armed interventions, an economic blockade and the cessation of trading relations. The party was isolated, fighting for its survival, desperate for support. But if the international revolution was not going to transpire in the immediate future, what now?

On top of the urgent need to resist the interventionists and win the civil war, the party soon came to realize that they would have to begin the process of building the 'lower' (socialism) and 'higher' (communism) phases on their own, and in the meantime work to make the international revolution happen, rather than wait for the historical conditions for it to ripen by themselves.

The task of promoting international revolution fell to a brand new body: Comintern or The Communist (Third) International. The founding Congress took place between 2 and 6 March 1919 in Moscow. The preparations had begun in January 1919 when there was a meeting of the representatives of communist parties and other left-wing groups. They adopted a manifesto: 'For the First Congress of the Communist International'. A total of 52 delegates arrived in February, and the Congress was opened on 2 March. Each delegate gave a report on the situation in their own land, and on 4 March they resolved to adopt the name 'Communist International'. They adopted a series of 21 propositions, including the necessity of proletarian revolutionary struggle to overthrow bourgeois governments (thus excluding the social-democratic parties in Western Europe from their ranks). From its beginnings Comintern was always caught in the paradoxical position of being an international movement run by a national communist party. This meant that the Leninist forms of communist organization were imposed upon communist parties elsewhere, and that communist parties were charged with working for revolution, and simultaneously defending the interests of the Soviet state.

The initial attempts at organizing revolutions and trying to impose a revolutionary government by force of arms in Poland in 1920 ended in miserable failure. After the rising of German communists failed in 1921, the focus of the Comintern shifted towards organizing to protect the interests of workers by forging an alliance with the moderate socialists, while at the same time trying to grow their membership and support among rank-and-file workers and trade unionists. This was the period often known as the 'United Front' epoch. It illustrates one of the surprising problems that dogged the Communist International: what attitude should they have towards their 'friends' (the moderate, reformist socialists)? The attitude towards their enemies was easy: implacable hostility. But how should they act towards the socialists? In theory there should have been common cause, if only on the basis that *my enemy's enemy is my friend*. However, the ideology of Comintern was that all social-democratic parties were really little more than the acceptable face of the bourgeoisie, and would, in the event of a revolutionary situation developing, inevitably betray the communists.

The United Front policy dissolved rapidly after the failed revolution in Germany in 1923, not least because socialists in Europe were wary of the intentions of the communists. The Great Depression of 1929 should have heralded an unparalleled opportunity for revolution, but the Soviets were so embroiled with their own internal transformation that Comintern missed the moment. In the early 1930s, the communists failed to halt the march of authoritarian right-wing regimes across Europe, by working to undermine the support and position of socialist parties. One of the terrible, ironic consequences of this was that these right-wing regimes proceeded to stamp out and persecute the communist parties, destroying many of the constituent members of Comintern.

A new policy emerged at the 7th Comintern Congress in August 1935. The march of fascism seemed to herald a threat not just to the communists in Europe but also to the USSR, and so this conditioned a shift towards the 'Popular Front' policy. This approach favoured an alliance between the communists and any group ready to stand against fascism or authoritarian anti-Soviet regimes. This led to the communists toning down the

Lev Davidovich Bronstein (Trotsky)

He was born on 26 October (7 November) 1879, son of a Jewish farmer, in the southern part of Ukraine. The family valued education highly, and when Lev was about nine years old they let him move to the city of Odessa, to stay with his 'uncle' and to go to school.

Lev was an exceptionally bright and capable student, and in 1896 he moved to Nicolayev to complete his secondary education and to study mathematics. This is where he began his revolutionary career. In 1897 he was instrumental in founding the South Russia Workers Union and he carried out a great deal of pamphleteering and propaganda work. However, in 1898 Lev was arrested for his political activities, put in prison, and in 1900 deported to Siberia. In 1902 he adopted the name Trotsky (the name of a former jailer from Odessa). In the split in the RSDLP in 1903, Trotsky initially sided with the Mensheviks against Lenin but in 1904 he became in his words a 'non-factional' social democrat.

He returned to Russia in 1905 and played a key role in the revolutionary events that year. He was arrested and put on trial in 1906, and was sentenced to exile for the rest of his life. He escaped to Vienna, and in 1914 he went to neutral Switzerland. When the February Revolution broke out, he was living in New York, and he finally made it back to Russia in May 1917. Trotsky played a formative role in the organization of the October uprising.

After the Revolution, he became People's Commissar for Foreign Affairs, and was responsible for the reorganization of the Red Army which led to the victory in the Civil War. After Lenin's death in 1924, Trotsky was gradually outmanoeuvered and marginalized by Stalin in the struggle for power. In October 1927 Stalin had Trotsky expelled from the Party Central Committee. He was eventually expelled from the USSR in February 1929.

He spent the rest of his time looking for a safe place to compose his critiques of Stalin. He spent four years in Turkey, two years in France, two years in Norway, before moving to Mexico in 1937. In 1938 Trotsky and his supporters founded the Fourth International, intended as a Trotskyist alternative to the Stalinist Comintern.

On 20 August 1940, Trotsky was attacked in his home by the Stalinist agent Ramon Mercader, who smashed a pickaxe into the back of Trotsky's head. He died the next day on 21 August 1940.

explicitly revolutionary and communist elements in their pro-grammes, and also created great dilemmas for communists in China and Spain, who felt betrayed by this policy. When Stalin concluded the Nazi–Soviet pact in 1939 to give the USSR a 'breathing-space', Comintern had become defunct. This was recognized as much by Leon Trotsky, who on 28 October 1938 set up the 'Fourth International' at a founding conference in New York, the aim of which was the 'full material and spiritual liberation of the toilers and exploited through the socialist revolution' and was dedicated to criticizing the actions of the Third International (Frank, 1979).

In 1943, Stalin decided to close Comintern. The wartime alliance between the USSR, Great Britain and the USA made Comintern a rather uncomfortable guest at the negotiating table. The wartime situation also meant it was almost impossible to coordinate the activities of communists on an international scale, and so Comintern was finished. On 15 May 1943 the Executive Committee issued the following proposal:

The Communist International, as the directing guiding centre of the international working-class movement, is to be dissolved, thus freeing the sections of the Communist International from their obligations

arising from the statutes and resolutions of the Congresses of the
Communist International. (Degras, 1971: 479)

Comintern had manifestly failed to promote the international
workers revolution. It is somewhat ironic that the rapid growth
of communism after the Second World War came after Comintern had ceased to function.

The overall record of Comintern between 1919 and its dissolution by Stalin in 1943 was at best mixed. The highly centralized
nature of Comintern made it very inflexible, often unable to
respond to the precise conditions in any country. The dominance
of the RCP was achieved at the expense of independent-minded
leaders of the national communist parties. Comintern's policy
altered on a whim, which did enormous damage to local communist parties. Finally, in the developing world it tended to support
anti-imperialist forces, even if they were decidedly unsympa-
thetic to left-wing values and ideals.

Building communism: politics, economics, society in the USSR 1917–53

The task of building communism at home seemed even more
daunting than the task of promoting an international revolution.
Economic collapse, cultural backwardness, international hostility,
social tensions and growing political estrangement all seemed
to suggest that this was an impossible job. So, how did the
Bolsheviks do in attempting this Herculean task of building
communism in the war-ravaged Russian land?

The communist 'model' envisaged, in the long run, a society
without politics and without a state: a participatory, democratic,

decentralized, self-governing system in which the administration of things would replace the government of men. This required a high level of education and communist consciousness among the people, an international arena dominated by communism (to prevent the need for an army to defend the communists from external intervention) and structures to promote the maximum possible participation by the people. To reach this goal though, a transitional period was required in which the old structures of power would be dismantled, which would allow the new shoots of the future communist system to emerge. The dismantling of the old structures began almost immediately, along with substantial measures to suppress the old classes and ensure that the revolution could not be overturned by the return of the bourgeoisie, the nobility, the generals and/or the clergy. In the period between October 1917 and July 1918, the organs of local and central government were dissolved, including the Constituent Assembly, the first ever national, popularly elected democratic assembly in Russian history, in January 1918. The process of dismantling and suppression was implemented through a new constitution which was adopted on 10 July 1918. This constitution gave a broad swathe of rights and privileges to the workers and peasants, many of which were denied to members of the 'old classes', including the right to vote. But the act of suppression was not confined to legislative initiatives. In December 1917, the All-Russian Extraordinary Commission for the Suppression of Counter-Revolutionary Sabotage and Speculation (*Cheka*) was created. This evolved into a political and economic police force, deploying repression and terror against perceived enemies of the state. The difficulty for the state, particularly when they were engaged in an all-out struggle for survival during the civil war, was that the 'legitimate' post-revolutionary function of suppressing the old classes quickly became a fairly indiscriminate use of terror against elements deemed to be 'anti-Soviet'. Right from the start, terror was woven into the fabric of the Soviet state. By the end of July 1918, the old system had been almost fully dismantled, or was in the process of being eroded, and the old classes were being neutralized.

Moves to create a new type of political system were handicapped from the outset by two things: lack of expertise and the Bolshevik instinctive preference for central control. Consequently, the aim of growing a system of governance that fostered popular participation and local, democratic organs of power was deeply compromised right from the start, without however disappearing entirely. The lack of expertise in governing required a mass crash programme of education to be undertaken in order to train the next generation of experts. In the meantime, this meant that the state had to rely upon the old 'experts': in the army, the economy, the administration, education and so on. The Red Army, formed by Trotsky, is a good example of this. The original post-revolutionary vision was of an army comprised of a democratic decentralized militia. This disappeared as the reality of the civil war imposed the need for urgent measures to ensure victory. The newly modelled Red Army replaced democracy with hierarchy, elections with appointments, and soldiers committees with old Tsarist officers. In order to ensure that the army remained staunchly Bolshevik, the party appointed political commissars – ideological watchdogs – to keep a weather eye on decisions taken.

This also highlights the other key point: the increased role of the party in the political system. The absence of expertise, and the low levels of communist consciousness among the people placed a huge premium on the party to maintain tight control over the transition to communism. Throughout the civil war period (1918–20) and beyond, the Communist Party gradually slipped into the centre of political life, controlling all decisions and appointments and accruing more and more power unto itself. In this way the dictatorship of the proletariat inexorably became the dictatorship of the party. The civil war context is often cited as one of the reasons why the Soviet state ended up as a one-party state. The desperate circumstances required ruthless measures to centralize control (and also to concentrate power) at the top of the system. While there is some credence to this view, it is only part of the story. Aside from the ruthless political culture of Bolshevism, the decision by the Bolshevik Party to seize power on their own in October 1917 was crucial. Having acted unilaterally then, it was always likely that this would result, eventually, in a monopoly of political power for the Communist Party. How did this monopoly come about?

The series of events which led to the emergence of a one-party state began in October 1917, and progressed most rapidly during the civil war when the non-Bolshevik socialists were gradually marginalized and excluded from the political life of the country. Gradually the ring of control became tighter and tighter. Bureaucratism and appointmentism replaced democracy, debate and election in the running of the system. Decision-making moved away from the Soviets (the local and national organs of popular representation) towards the party organs at all levels of the system. Power was concentrated increasingly at the centre and at the top. At the end of the civil war, the core elements of the Soviet political system were in place:

– a one-party political system;

– a centralized political system with little power for trade unions or Soviets;

– a political system that was heavily bureaucratized and hierarchical;

– a concentration of political power in the hands of a small elite;

– the selective use of terror as a means of government;

– extensive censorship and propaganda.

How did this develop after 1921?

The political developments between 1921 and 1953 saw very little substantive change to the core features outlined above. The party-state complex retained its exclusive hold on power. The levels of popular participation, democracy and accountability remained almost non-existent. The trends across the thirty years from the end of the civil war until Stalin's death in March 1953 were little more than an extension and deepening of central control, alongside periodic attempts to revive the class basis of the party and so retain its links with the proletariat.

The years 1921–28 mark the NEP period of Soviet history, which saw the last three years of Lenin's rule (he died in January 1924 after a series of strokes), followed by a succession struggle between Stalin, Trotsky, Bukharin et al. NEP was an economic arrangement which allowed for a degree of capitalist enterprise as a means of restoring the economy, and was seen as being something of a 'retreat', a 'breathing-space' before the advance to socialism and communism could be resumed. A retreat requires strict discipline though. So, the politics of NEP meant an **increase** in the powers of the centre, more dictatorial powers for the party, stricter ideological and political controls over society. The main difference between the NEP and the pre-NEP period was that, after 1921, controls were increasingly applied within the party itself. At the 10th Party Congress, the party imposed a ban on factions to prevent dissension within the party causing a split and leading to a weakening of the Soviet state. The other key initiative was the instigation of a purge of the ranks of the party. In order to try to maintain a proletarian essence in the party, the leadership sought to cleanse itself of 'careerist' elements, and to replace them with persons of a peasant or proletarian class origin. This not only tended to reinforce the powers of the centre, but also set the precedent that the party itself could contain 'undesirable' elements that would need to be removed.

After 1929, the leadership passed to Joseph Stalin who emerged victorious from his political struggles with Leon Trotsky and Nikolai Bukharin. Stalin presided over an era of profound social and economic transformation, accompanied by the vicious whirlwind of terror, famine, death and forced labour between 1932 and 1953. The political developments of the Stalin era took three main forms. First, the party was gradually eclipsed under Stalin by the increase in powers of the leader and also the secret police (now named the NKVD). Stalin gradually concentrated more and more power in his own hands, ruling through his own agencies and bodies and marginalizing the party. Politics became more personal and more dictatorial, culminating in the monstrous 'cult of personality', whereby Stalin became revered and deified as the all-seeing, all-knowing, all-wise leader or *vozhd*'. Secondly, the state vastly increased its controls over, and surveillance of, the population and of different professional and social groups. All groups were now forced to toe the party line. Thirdly, the process of purging the party was renewed with greater vigour and energy. This occurred in two waves. The first wave accompanied industrialization and the collectivization of agriculture between 1929 and 1932, as terror was unleashed on the peasantry and other specialists. The search was on for 'enemies' who were thought to be disrupting and obstructing the construction of the new communist paradise. The second wave began in 1936. It was prompted by the assassination of Sergei Kirov in December 1934 and the growing anxiety caused by the rise of National Socialism in Germany. The search for enemies and Fifth Columnists culminated in the hideous excesses of the 'Great Terror' of 1936–38, when vast numbers fell victim to the whims of Stalin and the NKVD, were arrested, interrogated and either sent off to exile, sent off to labour camps or executed. Terror had become institutionalized in the operation of the Soviet state (Sandle, 1999).

The period between 1939 and 1953 saw very little change. The picture painted here – personal dictatorship, terror, state control – continued to be an accurate depiction of Soviet reality. Although the 1936 Constitution proclaimed that the Soviet political system was awash with democratic rights and freedoms, they existed only on paper. The dictatorship of the proletariat as envisaged by Marx and Engels had metamorphosed into a terroristic dictatorship of Stalin, the NKVD and the Communist Party. In one sense, the Communist Party had clearly achieved part of their aims: to destroy the old state and to clear the rubble for the emergence of a new state through the construction of an authoritarian system that would suppress the old classes and defend the gains of the revolution. The problem was that no new shoots of an alternative political system – participatory, democratic, account-able, popular – could be seen. In fact, the state appeared to be growing more and more powerful with each year. The likelihood of a 'withering away' of the Soviet state seemed to be receding.

If we turn to the field of economics in the period 1917–53 then we can see a similar process at work: a successful elimination of the structures of the 'old regime', but a more problematic exer-cise in building the economic foundations of the new paradise. The key issues for the Bolsheviks were to transform ownership relations and to increase production. The abolition of two 'evils' – private ownership of the means of production, and scarcity – were firmly in the sights of the Bolshevik leadership. But what would a communist economy look like? What did an economy with socialized ownership of the means of production mean in practical terms? Should it be run by the state? The workers? The party? How would a planned economy work? How could an economic system be built in which labour time was reduced to a minimum, the division of labour was abolished, the free market had been surpassed by central planning, an abundance of mater-ial goods were being produced and money has disappeared?

The overriding Bolshevik imperative was to increase produc-tion. This underpinned the entire economic edifice that was constructed after 1917. In many cases this caused the party to amend or adjust its ideological preferences in order to ensure that production was maximized. The urgency to increase produc-tion was not just about economic stabilization or creating the basis for socialism. It was also a policy with an important polit-ical and ideological dimension. Increasing production meant a rapid increase in industrialization, and so a rapid growth in the numbers of industrial workers. This was essential if the party was to increase its levels of support in the country and so maintain itself in power.

In the immediate aftermath of the revolution, the Bolsheviks began the process of taking control of the economy. Steps to nationalize the economy emerged fitfully between October 1917 and June 1918. The process was a messy and complex one, as control of the factories was contested between the state, factory committees and private owners. The primary struggle was between the state – which favoured a centralized, hierarchical economic organization – and the factory committee movement – which favoured popular participation, decentralization and local self-management in the factories. The state triumphed, as it was seen as being the most effective mechanism to raise output. The victory of central control was sealed with the rapid expansion of the scope and powers of *Vesenkha* (The Supreme Economic Council), which had as its task the coordination of the economy. In the factory, control was shifted away from the workers and towards the appointed managers and technical experts. The abolition of private ownership of the means of production had, by and large, been carried out. It was replaced with nationalization, central control and state ownership, rather than popular ownership, local autonomy or workers' control (Sandle, 1999).

The policy during the civil war continued this trend of central control as a means of raising productivity. The state exercised strict control over the priorities of production, over the labour force and instituted a state trading monopoly which resulted in the administrative allocation of resources. Management in the factories was exercised by one person. In the chaotic conditions of the civil war, the collapse of the rouble led to the emergence of a moneyless economy. Wages had to be paid in kind. Some services in municipal areas were free, and money transactions were replaced by paper transactions. Some theorists, rather optimistically, assumed that this meant the country was on the verge of communism rather than the verge of chaos!

Agriculture was a deeply contested sphere. The Bolsheviks' long-term aim was to create large-scale collective farms or 'grain factories' which would be efficient, modern and technologically advanced. In the meantime they had to find ways to encourage production and cooperation, without encouraging the growth of capitalism in the countryside. In the conditions of the civil war, grain production and supply to the towns and the army proved deeply problematic, leading the Bolsheviks to favour coercive solutions, which caused a devastating famine in 1919/20, and consequently a huge gulf to appear between the party and the peasantry. At the end of the civil war, the crisis in food supply caused the Bolsheviks to undertake a radical reorientation of their agricultural policy.

One of the most significant developments of this period came in February 1920. A State Electrification Commission was formed to accelerate the process of electrification across the country. This was viewed as critical to the process of industrializing and modernizing Russia, and came to be seen as a highly potent symbol of the Bolshevik drive to take Russia from the darkness of backwardness and underdevelopment to the light of progress, modernity and technological advancement. At the 8th Congress of Soviets, Lenin said:

Communism is Soviet power plus the electrification of the whole country. Otherwise the country will remain a small peasant country . . . and we

must realise that only when the country has been electrified . . . shall we
be victorious . . . [and] our communist economic development will become
a model for a future socialist Europe and Asia. (Lenin, 1920: 519)

This process of trying to coordinate the electrification campaign
gave a huge impetus to the creation of a mechanism to plan the
economy, one of the key components of an economy which is
seeking to overcome the irrationality of capitalism and to dis-
tribute goods and services on a just and equitable basis. In April
1921 Gosplan (the State Planning Commission) was created.
Although the precise meaning of planning was unclear, the basic
position was clear: the Soviet economy was to be a centrally controlled, centrally planned one.

The end of the civil war enabled the Bolsheviks to take stock
and attempt to rebuild their devastated economy. In March 1921,
the party, prompted by Lenin, introduced the New Economic
Policy (NEP) (Nove, 1992). Realizing that the international
revolution was disappearing over the horizon, the focus shifted
to domestic developments. NEP extolled the virtues of a mixed
economy. It encouraged small producers to increase their output
of grain by levying a tax-in-kind on the peasants. Once this tax
had been levied, the peasants were free to dispose of the surplus
as they wished: either to market it, consume it themselves or
feed it to their livestock. This was a major departure from the
civil-war policy of forcible requisitioning of grain, and resulted in
a very rapid recovery of grain production and also a flourishing of
capitalism in the countryside: buying and selling, entrepreneurs,
market trading and a growth of economic activity between the
town and the countryside. At the same time, the Bolshevik
leadership were determined to limit the growth of capitalism,

by retaining state control of the key economic levers: banking, finance, foreign trade and the major industries remained in state hands. Some small and medium-sized firms were either leased to entrepreneurs or returned to private owners to enable them to produce for the market and to make a profit. The idea was to make the whole system more flexible, more consumer-oriented and better able to use expertise to rebuild the economy. This (partial) restoration of capitalist elements and practices accounts for the tightening of political controls, to ensure that political power did not flow to these new economic forces. NEP achieved its goal of restoring life to the economy and reviving economic production, and also brought peace and stability in the relationship between the Bolsheviks and the peasantry which had been so strained during the civil war. But how long was NEP to last for? A debate over NEP rumbled on in the party until Stalin's decisive break with NEP at the end of 1928. After Lenin's death, a debate engulfed the party over, first, who would replace Lenin as leader and, second, what was the best way to build socialism and communism in the USSR?

The transformation of the Soviet economic system was rapidly accelerated after 1929, when Stalin embarked on his policy of rapid industrialization and forced collectivization. The reasons for this Great Leap are manifold. Partly it was a response to the problems in the economy in 1928, when the peasants decided not to sell as much grain, as there was little to buy and the price of grain was quite low. This caused alarm in the party as it appeared to place in jeopardy the party's decision to push ahead with industrialization. A reliable supply of grain was essential if industrialization was to succeed. Partly it was a response to popular frustration: radicals were impatient to see progress towards communism. NEP seemed to be pandering to capitalism. Partly it was a realization of growing international hostility and danger. If the USSR did not industrialize quickly, could an attack from a hostile capitalist power be resisted? Finally, it was also caused by Stalin's personal calculation of his political interests. To defeat Bukharin in the struggle for the leadership, Stalin proposed a platform which favoured radicalism, energy and dramatic transformation within the national boundaries of Russia, as opposed to Bukharin's gradualist, pro-NEP road to socialism.

Iosif Vissionarich Djugashvili (Stalin)

He was born in Gori, Georgia, on 6 (18) December 1878. His father was a cobbler and a heavy drinker, who allegedly beat his son regularly. He attended a church school in Gori, and graduated top of his class and went to the Tiflis Theological seminary. Although his mother wanted him to become a priest, he attended the seminary because it offered the best educational opportunities in Georgia at the time.

He was expelled from the seminary for revolutionary activities in 1899, and worked in the revolutionary underground in the Caucasus for ten years as an activist, pamphleteer and occasional bank robber, under the pseudonym of Koba (a hero of the nineteenth-century Georgian independence movement). His first wife Ekaterina Svanidze died in 1907, leaving one son (Yakov). He married Nadezhda Alliluyeva in 1919. She died, in rather mysterious circumstances, in 1932 (she may have committed suicide). The couple had two children, Vassili and Svetlana.

He was appointed to the Bolshevik Central committee in 1912 by Lenin, and he adopted his revolutionary name Stalin ('Man of Steel') the following year. Although Stalin did not play a high-profile role in the events of 1917, he steadily worked his way up the party hierarchy, until by 1922 he occupied the key administrative post in the system: General-Secretary of the Party.

After Lenin's death, Stalin set about consolidating his grip on the reins of power until by 1929 he had become the undisputed leader of the USSR. In the 1930s he oversaw a whirlwind of social and economic change, and also instigated an epoch of terror and reprisals against real and imagined enemies. Millions benefited from increased educational opportunities. Millions died as a result of famine, exile, imprisonment and execution.

In 1939, Stalin signed a non-aggression pact with Hitler. This lasted only two years until June 1941 when the Nazis invaded. Stalin oversaw the brutal conflict and emerged triumphant. After the war Stalin undertook to rebuild the USSR and to create a buffer zone of sympathetic communist states in Eastern Europe to prevent any further invasions and to promote the international communist revolution. In his latter years, Stalin became increasingly suspicious. He died on 5 March 1953, probably of a cerebral haemorrhage (although the circumstances are still a little murky).

His body was removed from the Kremlin Wall in 1961 during Khrushchev's de-Stalinization drive.

The transformation was immense and immediate. The aim was to modernize and industrialize the Soviet economy as rapidly as possible, *on their own*. The economic policy of Stalin was designed to fuse the task of building the economic foundations of communism with promoting self-sufficiency. Rapid, coercive collectivization was launched in November 1929, halted briefly in the spring and summer of 1930 when it appeared that the spring sowings might not occur because of the chaos, and resumed again in 1931. By 1936, almost the whole agricultural sector had been collectivized, with farms becoming either *kolkhozy* (collective farms run by the farmers albeit with compulsory delivery quotas) or *sovkhozy* (state farms in which the

farmers received a guaranteed minimum wage). But this collectivization process was achieved at a terrible cost in human and
livestock terms. Millions died in Stalin's brutal campaign to prevent the rich peasants (*kulaks*) joining the collective farms, as
they were deemed to be ideological class enemies and so likely to
oppose the whole campaign. Countless peasants died in a dis-
tressing famine in Ukraine in 1932/33. Although the agricultural
sector had been collectivized by 1936, it bore little resemblance
to the vision of a series of modern, efficient, technologically
advanced grain factories in the countryside. The haste and
coercion which accompanied this campaign turned the collective
farms into inefficient institutions, with low incentives and
endemically low productivity.

In the industrial sector, the Stalinist transformation was
carried out via a series of 5-Year Plans, which promoted the heavy
industries: metal, coal, chemicals, energy. Plans were handed
down as a series of physical targets (i.e. supply x number of
widgets this week/month/year) to enterprises to fulfil. The focus
was upon haste and quantity: targets had to be over-fulfilled as
quickly as possible. Any lack of haste or shortfall in production
was deemed to be evidence of ideological laxity or deliberate
obstruction and could carry significant penalties. Consequently
the system was riddled with problems: shortages, bottlenecks,
poor quality, neglect of safety. Massive industrial complexes
sprang up across the country, literally transforming the land-
scape. The workers were subject to draconian labour laws, unless
they had been caught up into one of the forced labour camps
which undertook many projects in inhospitable conditions. The
whole process rested on a massive increase in the powers of the
state: it directed the allocation of labour and raw materials,

controlled the retail trade sector, fixed the prices for all consumer goods, and decided the targets and quotas for each industry and enterprise. A huge bureaucratic 'planning' apparatus was charged with overseeing this whole system. This system remained virtually unchanged until the advent of Mikhail Gorbachev in 1985 (Nove, 1992).

The economic structures built by Stalin superficially seemed to have fulfilled the criteria for a socialist economic system: industrialized, technologically modern, centrally planned, centrally controlled, having abolished the private ownership of the means of production. But the reality of the Stalinist economy was a long way from the nature of the economic system of socialism and communism. The economic system was inefficient, contradictory, irrational and rested on the exploitation and repression of the workers and the peasants. The Soviet economy may well have abolished private ownership and eliminated, in the main, the market as a means of distributing goods and services. But the Soviet economy in the 1930s and 1940s was in many ways an economy on a war footing rather than an economy advancing towards the egalitarian, socialized, materially abundant economy of communism.

In social terms, the Soviet system made very little headway in the attempt to construct a system of egalitarianism. This was not wholly unexpected though. The Bolsheviks subscribed to the orthodox Marxist viewpoint that absolute equality would only emerge with the advent of full-blown communism. Under communism, the policy of distribution 'according to need' would be manifest. In the transition from capitalism to communism, inequality would continue to exist but would gradually diminish. This would be distribution 'according to work done'. This was heightened in the Soviet case by the existence of competing imperatives. One strand of policy was to reduce the gap between the rulers and the ruled by implementing a rule whereby all officials received a working person's wage. The other strand of policy was to reward disproportionately experts and technical specialists to maximize their knowledge in the transitional era. In the period from 1917 to 1953, the latter imperative dominated, as the transition focused more upon the need to restore the economy and increase production, rather than working towards the egalitarian society of communism. This tendency reached its apogee under Stalin, when the idea of absolute egalitarianism was condemned as a 'petit-bourgeois' deviation. In its stead a whole edifice of inequality and privilege was constructed, favouring managers, military figures, party-state officials and key cultural figures over workers and peasants. But it is important to realize that these inequalities were nothing new for Bolshevism. It was purely the extent of inequality under Stalin which had increased in comparison with the 1917–29 period. In the fields of education and culture, the period 1917–53 saw a gradual diminution of radicalism and a return to traditionalism. This reflected the wider sense that, by the mid-1930s, the system had become committed to the defence and maintenance of what had been achieved, rather than pushing on towards communism. The Soviet system, born in radicalism and utopianism, had become deeply conservative.

Conclusion

What then shall we say about the Soviet experience of attempting to build communism after 1917? The first thing to note is that the task of destroying or negating elements of capitalism was carried out relatively swiftly and successfully. The retention of certain capitalist features can be traced to the peculiarities of the Russian context which required measures to overcome economic and cultural backwardness before the transition to socialism and communism could be embarked upon. The second part of this equation – constructing the foundations of socialism and communism – proved far more elusive. As the likelihood of an international proletarian revolution receded, the task of building socialism and communism became an internal domestic affair: 'socialism in one country'. While the Soviet Constitution of 1936 proclaimed that socialism had been built in the USSR, this was more of a celebration of the elimination of capitalism than a milestone on the road to the communist utopia. For while ownership of the means of production was no longer private, and the market had been all but eliminated, the system had signally failed to make any real progress towards the emancipation of the workers, and the creation of a society of freedom, equality, cooperation and justice. A façade or surface appearance of socialism had been constructed. But beneath this, the system was deeply inegalitarian and hierarchical. While the state had managed to improve the living standards of the masses – through education, electricity, housing and welfare – they remained in a situation of subordination and unfreedom, and on occasion subject to the random caprices of the Stalinist terror.

The Soviet theoretical interpretation of communism, and the Soviet experience of attempting to build communism became dominant because of the Soviet domination of the international communist movement. Alternative visions of communism did surface in the USSR throughout this period, most notably in the period 1917–23, when groups such as the Workers Opposition or the Kronstadt sailors attempted to place democracy, popular participation and the autonomy of the working masses at the heart of the operation of the Soviet system. These groups however were gradually suffocated as the power of the state grew inexorably across this period. After the Second World War, the proliferation of colonial liberation movements, the emergence of a Soviet bloc of countries in Eastern Europe and Asia, and the onset of the Cold War saw a rapid expansion of 'communist' countries. These countries looked to the USSR for leadership and support, and they adopted the Soviet 'model' of building communism. Thus the USSR began to export its ideals and its practices, which became a pattern for modernization for underdeveloped countries. This model was effective because it was able to mobilize scarce resources for a few key goals: economic modernization, defence and central control over the population. The model of building communism was in fact a model of modernization.

The Soviet system in the period 1917–53 was not a communist one. Even the ardent Stalinist ideologues would have accepted that. Were they on the road to communism though? In the two chapters that follow, we will examine the fate of the Soviet model of communism at home and abroad.

Recommended reading

The best introductions to the Soviet experience under Lenin and Stalin are as follows: G. Hosking, *A History of the Soviet Union* (Fontana, 1994); C. Read, *The Making and Breaking of the Soviet System* (Palgrave, 2001); M. Sandle, *A Short History of Soviet Socialism* (UCL Press, 1999).

The best specific pieces on the period 1917–53 and various aspects
of this era include: N. Bukharin and E. Preobrazhensky, *The ABC of
Communism* (Penguin, 1969); E.H. Carr, *The Bolshevik Revolution 1917–23*
[3 vols] (Penguin, 1966); C. Ward, *Stalin's Russia* (Arnold, 1999);
C. Read, *From Tsar to Soviets* (UCL Press, 1996); A. Nove, *An Economic
History of the USSR* (Penguin, 1992); A. Nove (ed.), *The Stalin Phenomenon*
(Weidenfeld & Nicolson, 1993). On Comintern, see J. Braunthal, *The
History of the International [vol. 2] 1914–43* (Nelson, 1967); J. Degras (ed.)
The Communist International 1919–43 [3 vols] (Cass, 1971); B. Lazitch
and M. Drachkovitch, *Lenin and the Comintern* (Hoover Institution Press,
1972); M. Lewin, *Russian Peasants and Soviet Power* (Allen & Unwin,
1968); J. Arch Getty and O. Naumov, *The Road to Terror* (Yale University
Press, 1999); E. van Ree, *The Political Thought of Joseph Stalin*
(RoutledgeCurzon, 2002).

CHAPTER 4

The decline and fall of communism in the USSR 1953–91

Introduction

STALIN SPENT THE LAST FEW YEARS of his life deftly avoiding the question of when the process of constructing the higher or final phase of communism should begin. He was aware that setting off down that road would inevitably entail substantial change in the way the system operated, if Marx's vision was to be realized. The party continued to profess in public their commitment to building communism. However, given the highly conservative orientation of the regime after 1945, the likelihood of setting off on the road to communism was always going to be slight. The death of Stalin in 1953 changed all that. The death of the dictator brought great uncertainty to the people and the surviving leaders of the USSR. How do you choose a successor to someone who had been depicted as a demigod? Who could be trusted? Should you continue to have one sole leader, or should there be a return to some form of collegial leadership? And what of the future? Where was the USSR headed? In the years after 1953, the successive leaders – Khrushchev, Brezhnev and Gorbachev – offered contrasting answers to this latter question. By 1991, the Communist Party under Gorbachev had explicitly abandoned the goal – central to the party's existence and identity since coming to power – of building a communist society according to Marx's blueprint. Two crises engulfed the USSR between 1953 and 1991: a crisis of faith (which manifested itself in the collapse of belief in communism) and a systemic crisis (which led to the collapse of the USSR in December 1991).

The crisis of faith 1953–91

Khrushchev and the redefinition of communism

When Stalin died, a leadership struggle took place which was only properly resolved in 1957 when Khrushchev (who had seemed the least likely of the leaders to succeed in 1953) became the pre-eminent figure. Part of Khrushchev's rise to power involved being the first person to reveal (highly selectively) some of the crimes and errors perpetrated by his former boss and colleague. In a four-hour 'secret speech' to a closed session of the 20th Party Congress in 1956, Khrushchev set out to detail various aspects of Stalin's rule. Apart from the personal moral benefits which he achieved by revealing these things, Khrushchev also inaugurated what has become known as the policy of de-Stalinization: an attempt to remove the worst excesses of Stalin's rule from the system, while retaining the key essential elements of the Soviet system intact (Khrushchev, 1971). This policy of de-Stalinization also encompassed the sphere of ideology, and led to moves to create a new party programme to replace the 1919 version which by this time had been rendered obsolete by the massive changes in the domestic and international arena. In spelling out the tasks facing the USSR in the new Party Programme, Khrushchev and those involved in the drafting had to grapple once more with the definitions and details of what 'communism' might look like.

Throughout the 1950s a series of drafts and proposals were discussed. Eventually a document was compiled which was submitted for nationwide discussion in 1961. It was discussed, approved and adopted at the 22nd Congress in October 1961. The most startling points contained in the new Party Programme were first the timetable for the construction of communism (no specific timetable had ever been published before) and also the details of what the communist society might look like. Previous programmes had dealt only in the generalities provided by Marx and Engels (CPSU, 1961).

The content of the 1961 Programme

In its preamble, the programme states that: 'Today the Communist Party of the Soviet Union is adopting its Third Programme, a programme for the building of communist society' (CPSU, 1961: 449). This was the most distinctive feature of the Programme. Socialism 'had triumphed fully and finally in the USSR' and so the USSR had now entered a new stage: the full-scale construction of communism. Dividing the period 1961–80 into two decades, the Programme asserted that, by 1980, a 'communist society on the whole will be built in the USSR'. The Programme ended with the bold declaration:

THE PARTY SOLEMNLY PROCLAIMS: THE PRESENT GENERATION SHALL LIVE UNDER COMMUNISM! (CPSU, 1961: 545)

Compared with its predecessors, the 1961 Programme was a far more detailed and weighty document. It was split into two sections. The first was concerned with the global transition from capitalism to communism, the second with the construction of a fully communist society in the USSR. There were some new elements in here. The opening section on global developments broke new ground in several areas. Khrushchev's notion of peaceful coexistence with capitalism was accompanied by two further innovations which radically transformed the Soviet view of the spatial and temporal relationship between capitalism and communism. The first was that there were many roads to socialism (and it need not necessarily be a violent revolutionary one). The other was that wars were no longer inevitable.

The second section also contained substantial doctrinal innovations. Khrushchev now argued that 'the dictatorship of the proletariat had fulfilled its historic mission.' This was a key point. It was now affirmed that the state had become an 'All-People's State' (CPSU, 1961: 547). Orthodox Marxist theory argued that the state was always an instrument through which one class ruled. Khrushchev substantially revised this doctrine by arguing that the state now represented the interests of the Soviet people as a whole. The other main innovation was the specific timetable for the construction of communism. Khrushchev outlined that communism would be built in two stages. From 1961 to 1980, the USSR would surpass the West and create the material–technical basis for communism. By 1980, communism would 'on the whole' or 'in the main' be built. Full or complete communism would be constructed in the subsequent period (1980 onwards, although there was no timetable specified). The ultimate end point of final communism was postponed long into the future. The immediate task set by the Third Party Programme was the construction of the material–technical basis of communism. But this was not the 'final' communist society as envisaged by Marx and Engels. So what type of communist society did Khrushchev have in mind?

The central plank of Khrushchev's vision of communism was that there would be an 'abundance of material and cultural wealth'. This would be achieved through massive increases in both economic output (industrial and agricultural) and labour productivity between 1961 and 1980. The details of this abundance included a massive increase in the availability of consumer goods, food produce and housing for the Soviet people. In addition there would be a plethora of social and economic benefits for the Soviet people, including:

- the shortest working day/week in the world;

- free lunches in schools, offices, factories etc.;

- pensions and health care extended to collective farmers;

- free public transport and so on (CPSU, 1961: 545).

In 1961, this amounted to a massive advance in the living standards of the Soviet people. But this was not material abundance as Marx and Engels would have understood it. This was not the abolition of scarcity, but the attempt to achieve a western level of consumption: ambitious by Soviet standards, but hardly akin to a utopian society. The full abolition of scarcity would only arrive later. Khrushchev appears to have redefined Lenin's dictum. Now, communism = western levels of consumption + welfare provision. This was a conservative, pragmatic vision of communism, little more than a more efficient version of the present. All of the radical changes – for instance the abolition of money – were to be reserved for the distant future.

In socio-political terms, the Programme was similarly cautious. Although the aim was to create a classless society by 1980, this was not one which had abolished inequality or social differentiation (which again was postponed until the latter phase of communism). In political terms, there was no notion of the state *withering away*. The CPSU itself would continue to play a central role in guiding and directing Soviet society. The concept of popular self-government was again postponed until the final stage of communism. The society which they labelled 'communism in the main' does appear to be a significant departure from the traditional Marxist view. Khrushchev had redefined communism by dividing it in two: a 'pragmatic' communism (up to 1980) in which there would still be commodity–money relations, a state and class distinctions; and a 'traditional' Marxist communism (a long time after 1980) which consisted of all the unrealizable, 'utopian' elements. In addition, even the ambitious and optimistic short-term aims of achieving communist society 'in the main' by 1980 were hedged in and heavily qualified, giving the leadership convenient scapegoats in the event of failure to achieve this target. On the whole, Khrushchev's vision does indeed appear to be rhetorically bold, but specifically pragmatic and rather conservative. Why?

Khrushchev wished to bolster his own authority by arguing for embarking on the construction of communism, and so supplanting the achievements of Stalin who had 'merely' achieved the construction of socialism by 1936. However, there was also an international dimension. Given the recent disputes with Yugoslavia and China, the socialist bloc was moving towards a degree of polycentrism. Being the first communist state to embark upon the construction of communism demonstrated the leading role of the USSR in the international socialist camp. Yet the reality of the Soviet economic system, and the need to maintain the party in power meant that the immediate tasks were little more than a continuation of existing policies and priorities. The 'material–technical basis of communism by 1980' had to be realizable (to maintain the legitimacy of the party) and non-disruptive (to maintain the party in power). Hence the disparity between the bold rhetoric about the future and the rather tame view of the intermediate period. Khrushchev subtly redefined communism to make it achievable, but in so doing stripped it of all the elements that Marx and Engels, Bukharin and Preobrazhensky identified as central to it. How did Khrushchev's successors cope with his bold promises?

Brezhnev: the postponement of communism

The removal of Khrushchev from power in October 1964 resulted in a joint leadership between Leonid Brezhnev and Aleksei Kosygin. One factor in the removal of Khrushchev was his constant tinkering and meddling which alienated many key people in the system, leaving him with little support. Brezhnev and Kosygin were charged with attempting to bring stability to the system, to overturn the unsettling changes introduced by Khrushchev. Part of this process of 'de-Khrushchevization' meant grappling with the bold rhetoric of Khrushchev's Party Programme: that communism would be built by 1980. The Brezhnev leadership responded to this by elaborating a new ideological concept: Developed Socialism (Sandle, 2002).

The official inauguration of this new concept occurred at the 24th Congress of the CPSU in March 1971 when Leonid Brezhnev talked about the notion of a developed socialist society having been built in the USSR. In 1967, Brezhnev had affirmed in a speech to mark the 50th anniversary of the October Revolution that the USSR was still in the process of 'the full-scale construction of communism', continuing the approach of Khrushchev. Four years later, the references to this ideal had all but disappeared. In its stead stood Developed Socialism. Why? Aside from Brezhnev's personal quest for prestige and credibility as a Marxist–Leninist theorist, there was a growing unease with the grandiose promises of Khrushchev's timetable. Yet they could not abandon the idea of making the transition to communism, as this was the entire *raison d'être* of the rule of the CPSU. A new interpretation was required. In addition, the CPSU had to maintain its pre-eminent position within the socialist bloc. If the USSR was no longer engaged in the construction of communism, on what basis could it claim to be the dominant state in the socialist bloc? All the countries were 'socialist'. Developed Socialism became a means of differentiating the USSR from the other socialist countries, while asserting its leading role: it was the first state to complete the construction of a 'developed socialist' society. For Brezhnev and others, socialism ceased to be a brief transitional period between capitalism and communism. It was a long historical phase, marked by its own laws of social development, not all of which had been revealed by the unfolding of the historical process. The transition to communism would now be a prolonged, gradual process. Communism by 1980 had been quietly abandoned. Socialism was becoming less of a transitional stage between capitalism and communism, and more of an historical stage in its own right.

A trend began to become apparent by the early 1970s whereby the Soviet state was continually postponing the realization of the final communist utopia further and further into the future. Long gone were the heady days of the civil war, the 1930s or the late 1950s when there was a genuine sense that they were on the verge of a breakthrough on the road to communism. Why was this? The gradual postponement of communism into the future occurred for a variety of reasons. The slowdown in economic performance and the seeming imperviousness of Soviet citizens to party propaganda brought a sense of pessimism into Soviet prognoses. Progress was slow and decelerating. At the same time capitalism was proving to be frustratingly resilient, undermining the core part of their ideological framework that capitalism was due to die out and be replaced by communism.

Perhaps the key factor was that the party and the system had undergone a subtle yet significant transformation: from being a revolutionary party designed and dedicated to making a revolution and transforming the world, it had become a ruling party, institutionalized, present- rather than future-minded, a force for conserving not transforming. This made the Communist Party more intent on maintaining and perfecting what they already had, rather than looking to build the utopia. In addition, this attracted people who were less revolutionary and more careerist in orientation. The gradual displacement of the utopian impulse from the words and discourse of the party meant that communism was becoming less and less prominent in party ideology and proclamation. This was mirrored by a gradual but notable shift in the outlook and values of the party members themselves. Anecdotally, it would appear that the proportion of people working in the system who were self-professed 'believers' began to decline in the 1960s and never stopped. Even those who dedicated their lives to persuading and motivating people to sacrifice themselves for the building of the communist utopia appeared to be doing little more than 'going through the motions' (Feifer, 1975). Belief in communism was fading. It was, however, still the ostensible goal and *raison d'être* of the party. After 1985, even this was to change.

Gorbachev: the abandonment of communism

The death of Brezhnev in November 1982 was followed very quickly by the deaths of the frail and elderly Yuri Andropov (1984) and Konstantin Chernenko (1985). In March 1985, Mikhail Gorbachev came to power. He proved to be a radical figure, in marked contrast to his immediate predecessors. His policies of *perestroika*, *glasnost* and democratization at home, and his espousal of a radical new foreign policy of unilateral arms cuts and withdrawal from Eastern Europe heralded an epoch of unprecedented global change, both in scope and speed. One by one Gorbachev undermined and removed the central pillars of Soviet ideology and Soviet political and economic practice: the one-party state; state ownership of the means of production; the prohibitions on the operation of the free market. Inexorably, attention turned towards the centrepiece of Marxist–Leninist ideology: communism. In the autumn of 1988, Soviet theorists nervously began to question the dominant understanding of 'socialism' in Soviet discourse. By the summer of 1991, communism had to all intents and purposes been discarded from the party's political vocabulary. How and why did this take place?

The theoretical renewal under Gorbachev began, like Brezhnev's, by reacting against the ideas of his predecessor. Gorbachev oversaw the drafting of a revised Third Party Programme, which was published in 1986, and which took the concept of Developed Socialism to task. Gorbachev, in addressing the 27th Congress of the CPSU in February 1986, attacked both Khrushchev's timetable and also Developed Socialism in one savage blow. Khrushchev's transition to communism? Simplistic. Brezhnev's concept of Developed Socialism? Unacceptable (Gorbachev, 1986). Why?

Gorbachev's reforms to the Soviet system were based on two fundamental premises: realism not utopianism, and pragmatism not dogmatism. The Soviet system was approaching crisis point, and this required radical measures to address these problems. In the course of 1987 and 1988, it became apparent to Gorbachev and other reformers that socialism Soviet-style was in large part responsible for this crisis. A search ensued for a renewed conception of socialism. This search turned up nothing though. Indeed the search was abandoned, and communism deemed to be an illusion. How did this happen?

The first inklings of a shift in thinking came in the international sphere. Gorbachev outlined a new approach to international relations and public diplomacy. His emphasis was centred on the need to promote tolerance, diversity, and dialogue between capitalism and socialism, and to prioritize common human values over class values. The stated rationale for this was the danger of imminent global destruction – either through nuclear war, nuclear accident or environmental catastrophe – and the need for all peoples and states of whatever political hue to cooperate to avoid this. The logic of this position was to undermine the notion that the world was divided into two camps: socialist and capitalist. Capitalism and socialism could learn from each other. Not every-thing 'capitalist' was bad. Not everything socialist was inher-ently 'good'. The implications of this were momentous. At one stroke it undermined one of the key pillars of the Marxist view of the world: that socialism was inherently superior to capitalism, and was inevitably going to succeed and replace capitalism. Soviet ideology no longer proclaimed that socialism was the inevitable future for all capitalist countries. The unbroken progress of history – through capitalism to socialism and ultimately com-munism – could no longer be sustained (Shenfield, 1987).

Inexorably, ideological innovations in the international sphere began to reverberate at home. A prolonged academic debate about what a 'renewed' Soviet socialism might look like began in the autumn of 1988, and surfaced in the public arena a year later when Gorbachev published his statement of faith 'The Socialist Idea and Revolutionary *Perestroika*' in November 1989 (Gorbachev, 1989). There Gorbachev unveiled his new big idea: *humane demo-cratic socialism*. Gorbachev's vision of socialism was an eclectic mixture of general world experience, national peculiarities, a rereading of Marx and Lenin, and importing elements of European social democracy. No longer was it to be guided by the principle 'if it's not capitalism, it must be socialism'. Elements that were previously defined as 'capitalist' – the free market, private ownership of the means of production – were now legitimately 'socialist'. The organizing themes of Gorbachev's vision were ethical: humanism, morality, the individual, freedom, democracy, pluralism, consumerism, creativity. The old Soviet notions of socialism were 'scientific' and structural: statist, productivist, collectivist, class-based. Gorbachev was attempting to reconcile competing imperatives: to break with certain elements from the past, to create a society that could respond to the social, political and economic challenges of rapid technological changes, and to retain a recognizably socialist vision. While he almost managed to do the first two, the latter proved pretty much beyond him (Sandle, 1999). With the publication of the draft Party Programme of July 1991, Soviet socialism had been reduced to a watered-down version of European social democracy, or something akin to welfare capitalism. Gorbachev managed to hijack the draft Party Programme and turn it into a personal statement of faith by bypassing the official drafting commission. This programme acknowledged the abandonment of a belief in the future communist society: stateless, classless, harmonious and free from exploitation. Communism ceased to be the ostensible goal towards which the Soviet system was moving. De facto the CPSU had abandoned its commitment to, and belief in, orthodox Marxism–Leninism. The belief system of the CPSU was now essentially similar to those of West European social-democratic parties. The Bolshevik programme – to transform the world – was finally laid to rest. With it died a belief in the attempt to realize communism Soviet-style (Sandle, 1996).

All three of the post-Stalin leaders had reacted very differently when confronted with the problem of what to do about constructing a communist society in the USSR. Khrushchev redefined it. Brezhnev postponed it indefinitely. Gorbachev abandoned it. It was not just belief in the communist idea that collapsed in 1991 though. The system designed to build communism also fell apart. So what were the reasons for this?

The crisis of the communist system 1953–91

The collapse of the communist systems in Eastern Europe in 1989 and the USSR in 1991 brought the curtain down on the experiment to attempt to shape a society according to the ideas of Marx and Engels. Yet the decline of this system had set in much earlier. In fact, the system constructed by Stalin in the 1930s remained pretty much intact, albeit with slight adjustments and modifications right up until 1991. Observing the period between the death of Stalin and the death of the Soviet system in 1991, it is interesting to note that the performance and vitality of the system declined in almost direct proportion to the erosion of belief in the ideal of communism as the end point towards which the Soviet system was moving. This was no real surprise. The system was set up to achieve a goal. Once belief in that goal began to dissolve, so doubts began to appear in people's minds. Doubts raised questions about legitimacy and credibility, and before long the ruled no longer believed in the rulers. As the system began to lose its *raison d'être*, it also began to lose its legitimacy in the eyes of the people. Herein lies one of the key reasons for the decline and fall of the communist regimes in the late twentieth century.

One of the reasons why people began to lose faith in the system was because of the performance of the system. As the rule of the Communist Party rested not on a democratic basis of legitimacy, but on its ability to demonstrate publicly and practically that the Soviet system was moving towards socialism and communism, then the questions about the ultimate goal towards which the system was moving could have been deflected by evidence that capitalism was on the wane and that the communist system was in all respects superior. Unfortunately, the period after 1953 showed that capitalism was more resilient than Soviet theorists had anticipated, and that the Soviet economy was struggling to achieve its objectives. This is not to say that the capitalist system performed particularly well in this period. It didn't. The exploitation of the Developing World, the ravaging of the environment, the massive levels of unemployment, poverty and global debt all testify to a system that was doing massive damage to the welfare of the people and the planet. However, the fact that capitalism continued to exist and was able to demonstrate technological superiority over the communist regimes was enough to undermine one of the key planks of communist dogma: that capitalism was on the way out. It is also the case that the Soviet economy, even into the 1970s, continued to show reasonable levels of growth. The problem was that growth was *slowing down* (and eventually by the late 1970s and early 1980s had stopped and even gone into reverse). Why did the performance of the system start to decline?

The economic system built by Stalin was essentially designed, like a wartime economy, to achieve a few basic aims very rapidly – in this case, to modernize and industrialize. But it was riddled with problems. Problems in the system – including economic inefficiency, bureaucratization, waste, shortages, bottlenecks and poor quality – were exacerbated by declining enthusiasm among the people, ideological dogmatism and corruption among the elite. Having achieved the aims for which it was built, and survived the trauma of the Nazi invasion, it then proved incredibly difficult to adapt this economic system to the demands of a modern, industrial, technological consumer-led society. Problems accumulated and proved impossible to solve. The advent of the Cold War meant that resources also had to be pumped into the military sphere, draining the domestic economy of much needed money and materials. All in all, the period after the death of Stalin was one of maintaining the system that had already been built, and the edifice of power and privilege for the elite which accompanied it, rather than transforming the system in order to usher in the golden era of communism. The USSR continued to be a global superpower in this era, but the seeds of its demise had already been sown. In spite of its military prowess, its nuclear capability and its achievements in space exploration, the inability of the CPSU both to solve the problems inherent in the operation of the Stalinist system and to transform its modus operandi fatally undermined the long-term viability of the Soviet system. This had far-reaching social, political and international repercussions.

This combination of a corrupt, repressive political system, privileged unaccountable elite, a heavily censored press and media, an economic system with low incentives for workers and consumer goods both in short supply and of variable quality, and a loss of faith created a populace high on cynicism and apathy, alienated and immune to the rhetoric. Endless queuing became a way of life. Drunkenness was the main coping mechanism. Bribery was accepted as the normal way to get things that were unavailable. Either that or pilfer from the state. In political terms, the elite became increasingly divorced from the masses, interested solely in the preservation of their own position and privileges and in repressing dissident or critical voices. As the system began to decline, so the communist 'model' in the USSR became less and less attractive as the preferred system of choice for the discerning post-colonial leader. Khrushchev, Brezhnev and Gorbachev all tried, in vain, to arrest this decline.

Charting the decline

The Khrushchevite era (1953–64) has been designated as one of de-Stalinization: a clear move away from the Stalinist approach. Yet the continuities between Stalin and Khrushchev are as notable as the changes. Certain elements were abandoned by Khrushchev, most notably the 'cult of personality', the one-person dictatorship and the use of mass, arbitrary, random terror against the population as a method of rule. However, the core elements of the Soviet 'model' remained:

– central planning;

– state ownership;

– priority of heavy industrial development;

– one-party state (Sandle, 1999; Filtzer, 1993).

What changed after 1956 was the way in which these different elements worked in practice. The basic operation of the system changed very little. But gradually Khrushchev introduced adjustments and reforms in an attempt to revitalize the system and restore its dynamism. He was also concerned to prevent a return to mass terror. The deadening effect of the dictatorship of Stalin had stifled creativity and initiative, instilling fear and insecurity and fostering an atmosphere of suspicion and mistrust. If the Soviet system was to respond to the challenges of post-war reconstruction and continue to modernize and become a fully fledged, highly developed industrial economy, then changes had to be made to the Stalinist approach.

Probably the best illustration of the way in which Khrushchev sought to break with certain parts of the Stalinist approach, and yet retain other parts, is the speech that he made to the 20th Party Congress in February 1956. Khrushchev was aware of the fact that people were beginning to discuss the crimes, arrests and killings perpetrated under Stalin, and he felt it was necessary – for his own political position and also to defend the party – to raise this issue and pin all the blame on Stalin for everything, thus exonerating himself and the party from any culpability. It was a bold move, which could have backfired on him. In a four-hour speech Khrushchev selectively outlined a variety of crimes committed by Stalin. Blaming Stalin not only let Khrushchev and his fellow leaders off the hook, but it also had the added benefit of saying that the problems in the system were not endemic to the system itself. In other words the house was sound; it was just the former occupant who had caused all the problems. This inaugurated a campaign to remove evidence of Stalin from public life: statues, street names, place names, culminating in the re-moval of his body from the Kremlin Wall in 1961. Khrushchev's reforms were designed to revitalize the system built by Stalin though, rather than to destroy it.

The most notable changes introduced by Khrushchev were in the fields of socio-political practice and foreign policy. In the political arena, one of the most crucial changes was the sub-ordination of the secret police to the party, and the restoration of the party as the pre-eminent political institution. The Stalinist dictatorship had rested on the organs of terror to carry out its tasks. Now Khrushchev decided the party should return to its pre-1936 position. The NKVD was renamed the KGB (Committee of State Security) and placed under the control of the Party Central Committee. Many of its judicial functions were removed, and the whole edifice of terror was massively scaled down (without ever disappearing completely). Having restored the party, Khrushchev turned to the area of legality. Moves to create a system based on the rule of law were introduced, although in practice the party always remained well above the law. Greater autonomy in cultural affairs was extended to certain artists, writers and musicians. Reforms to the educational system were introduced to increase access to education for those from worker or peasant background. Housing stock was increased and welfare provision upgraded. Overall, the changes introduced by Khrushchev sought to make the system fairer, more predictable, more attuned to the interests of the consumer, yet without disturbing the fundamental distribution of power in the system (Sandle, 1999).

In the economic sphere, Khrushchev's changes were designed to improve the efficiency of the system. He aimed to decentralize the operation of the economy by creating regional economic councils which would coordinate the entire economic activity of a particular area or region. These councils were supposed to make the economic decision-making more closely related to the economic needs of the region. Their impact was almost entirely negligible, as the problems at central level were now duplicated at local level. The only really successful changes introduced by Khrushchev were the attempts to balance economic output more evenly between agriculture, heavy industry and consumer goods industries. Although the consumer had a higher priority, the system was still primarily geared to the heavy industrial sector (Nove, 1992).

The international policy of Khrushchev was shaped by two contexts: the growth of the Cold War, and the emergence of an international socialist bloc. The global competition between capitalism and socialism was fought on a variety of fronts: economic, military, ideological, cultural and sporting. The whole thrust of Khrushchev's approach to the international sphere was based on establishing supremacy over the USA, however that might be measured. The public rhetoric of Khrushchev announced a policy of 'peaceful coexistence' with the capitalist powers. But the expectation among the Soviet leaders was the same: that communism would supersede capitalism. The Soviet state embarked on a massive programme of military build-up, focusing upon nuclear weapons as part of its campaign to assert its supremacy over the capitalist powers. The launch of Sputnik in 1957 and the flight of Yuri Gagarin were all part of this sustained attempt to demonstrate the superiority of the Soviet system. This was accompanied by the policy of seeking out partner regimes in the newly liberated colonies in Africa, Asia and Latin America. The rise of Marxist–Leninist regimes in the developing world was another part of the war with capitalism. As the number of states owing their allegiance to the USSR grew, so it appeared that the world was turning Red in line with the predictions of Marx and Engels. The effect was short-lived and costly though. These states proved a drain on the Soviet economy and were not always the most reliable of partners. The international prestige and hegemony of the USSR also came under increasing threat with the dispute between Mao and Khrushchev leading to the emergence of China as a state to rival the USSR for leadership of the Soviet bloc (Kennedy-Pipe, 1998).

The combined effect of Khrushchev's reforms were quite mixed. Some improvements in living standards for the population, a cultural thaw entailing fewer restrictions in some cultural areas and a reduction in the use of terror were offset by continued economic problems, organizational chaos alongside an aggressive campaign against religion and religious believers. From 1959 onwards, Khrushchev was increasingly beleaguered as his opponents in the Politburo began to organize to try to get rid of him. Khrushchev's political authority began to wane as his policy failures began to mount. He also managed to alienate the key political constituencies in the system – the military and the party-state – through his reorganizations and reshuffling. By 1964, Khrushchev was left virtually without support, and he was removed by a palace coup in October 1964. He was pensioned off and died in relative obscurity in 1971 and his body buried in the Novodevichy Cemetery in Moscow (Taubman, 2002).

Khrushchev left two highly significant legacies, however. First, the fact that he was removed peacefully from power brought about something of a 'normalization' of Soviet politics, and particularly the succession process. Soviet elite politics, unlike under Stalin, was now much more regular, predictable and safe. Political rivals no longer needed to fear for their lives if they lost out in a political dispute. Secondly, the model of attempting to bring about reform through a policy of controlled liberalization served as an example for the Gorbachev generation who grew up under Khrushchev.

Nikita Sergeevich Khrushchev

He was born on 17 April 1894 to an illiterate peasant family in Kalinovka. He began working at an early age. In 1908 because of poverty they moved to Donetsk in Ukraine. It was the beginning of his activist career: at the age of 18, Khrushchev joined a group of workers who had organized a strike protesting about working conditions. He was fired. In 1914 he married his first wife Evfrosin'ia Ivanovna Pisareva. They had a daughter Julia (born in 1915) and a son Leonid (born in 1917).

Khrushchev found another job but continued his activism, helping to organize strikes in 1915 and 1916. In 1918 Khrushchev joined the Bolshevik Party and he fought in the Red Army in the Russian Civil War, serving as a political commissar. His wife died some time in 1919/20. He set up home with Nina Kukarchuk in 1924. Khrushchev gradually worked his way up the Ukrainian party hierarchy in the 1920s until in 1929 he got permission to go to Moscow to study in the Industrial Academy.

In 1934 he joined the Party Central Committee. In 1935 he became First Secretary of the Moscow City Committee and in 1939 he joined the Politburo. During the Great Patriotic War (1941–45) he served as a political commissar, most notably in the Battle of Stalingrad in 1942.

Khrushchev unexpectedly became the pre-eminent figure in the USSR after Stalin's death. He rose to become General-Secretary of the Party, and used the XXth Congress of the CPSU in February 1956 to launch a four-hour 'Secret' Speech to astonished party members whereby he denounced Stalin and his crimes (thereby exonerating himself from any blame for anything that happened between 1929 and 1953). Between 1956 and 1964 he undertook a series of high-profile campaigns to de-Stalinize the system, including agricultural reforms, massively increasing the housing stock, and bringing a halt to mass, random terror. He started the Soviet space programme.

In foreign affairs Khrushchev oversaw the invasion of Hungary in 1956, closed the border around West Berlin in 1961, and was a central figure in the Cuban Missile Crisis in 1962. After a series of policy failures he was removed from power in 1964, peacefully. He was the first Soviet leader not to die in post. He had a heart attack and died on 11 September 1971. He is buried in the Novodevichy cemetery in Moscow.

The regime which took over from Khrushchev was headed initially by Leonid Brezhnev and Aleksei Kosygin (Bacon & Sandle, 2002). Their approach was very similar to that of Khrushchev with two major differences: stability rather than change was to be the key, and the partial rehabilitation of Stalin. They had been brought to power to put a halt to the endless organizational changes of Khrushchev, and they did this by inaugurating a policy of 'trust-in-cadres': the state would allow the officials to govern in return for cooperation in securing the regime's goals. The upshot, however, was drift, stagnation and corruption. Local party officials were allowed to turn their part of the country almost into personal fiefdoms. Bribery and extortion grew. Turnover among the elite virtually ground to a halt. Two terms were coined to describe the Brezhnev era: *kleptocracy* (rule by thieves) and *gerontocracy* (rule by the aged). The more conservative bent of the Brezhnev regime was reflected in its partial rehabilitation of Stalin, in its rather draconian dealings with Eastern European communists and in a cultural clampdown at home.

The stirrings of protest and a desire for autonomy among the satellite states in Eastern Europe had first surfaced in the 1950s in East Germany, Poland and Hungary. In 1968, a reform movement in Czechoslovakia led by Aleksander Dubcek sought to liberalize and humanize the operation of the system. This movement – known as the Prague Spring – was brutally crushed by the military, and a clear message was sent about the limits of acceptable criticism. A similar clampdown occurred at home. The rise of the dissident movement in the mid-1960s – an underground network of individuals critical of the infringement of civil and human rights by the Soviet state – was met with unyielding repression, arrest and imprisonment. The thaw was over. A deep chill set in.

In many other respects, the Brezhnev regime maintained the Khrushchevite approach: strong emphasis upon the military, more balanced approach to economic development, selective use of terror, maintenance of the core institutions of the Soviet system (one-party state, central planning, etc.) and the continued attempts to outdo capitalism internationally, either through the cultivation of Third World client states or through competition in the sporting arena or in space. The period between 1964 and 1977 did see some minor reforms in the economic sphere, along with the unveiling, to a great fanfare, of a new Soviet constitution, replacing the 1936 Stalin constitution. Like its predecessor, it looked great on paper but meant little in practice. The period between 1977 and 1985 was a time of drift, decay, immobility and stagnation. The whole system seemed to be symbiotically linked to the health of a succession of ailing, aged leaders. Problems accumulated and were not dealt with. Corruption reached new heights (or depths). Cynicism and apathy were rife, summed up nicely by this old Soviet adage:

> There's no unemployment, yet nobody works.
> Nobody works, yet the plan still gets fulfilled.
> The plan gets fulfilled, yet there's still nothing in the shops.
> There's nothing in the shops, yet every fridge is full.

Every fridge is full, yet everyone still complains.
Everyone complains, yet the same people keep getting elected.

Brezhnev's death was swiftly followed by the deaths of Andropov in 1984 (who had started a drive against corruption) and Chernenko in 1985. Just prior to his accession, the new leader Mikhail Gorbachev was walking in the garden with his wife and uttered the phrase 'we cannot go on living like this'. It was to herald a period of unprecedented change, and ultimately the end of communism in the USSR.

The end of the USSR

The Gorbachev era witnessed a rapidly accelerating programme designed to reform, modernize and strengthen the Soviet system and in so doing enhance the position and legitimacy of the CPSU. Unfortunately for Gorbachev it accelerated wildly out of control, unleashed forces it had no way of stopping and ended by destroying that which it sought to transform. Gorbachev's programme of reform went through a series of different approaches, each one more radical than the last (Brown, 1996). Underpinning Gorbachev's initial approach was a synthesis of the ideas advocated by Khrushchev and Andropov. Gorbachev sought to liberalize the system, mobilize the people behind the reforms and squeeze more out of the system by clamping down on corruption and exhorting the populace to work harder. The central plank of Gorbachev's early reforms was the policy of *glasnost*: a more liberal approach to information and opinion, encouraging people to speak out, to criticize and to support the changes. The state gradually relaxed its censorship of the press, media and literature, and another, more prolonged cultural thaw set in. It was however something of a double-edged sword for Gorbachev, for while it had the effect of increasing popular participation and providing a voice for society, it also proved notoriously difficult to control. People and groups began to speak out not just in favour of Gorbachev and his policies, but also in support of their own interests: national autonomy, historical truth, environmental change. It was the first sign that society was stirring. Pluralism had arrived.

From 1986 to 1988, Gorbachev instituted a series of economic and political changes known as *perestroika* (restructuring). The aim was to provide more autonomy and flexibility in the economy, and to democratize the political system to give the people more of a voice. Inexorably these changes developed a momentum of their own. Democracy within the Party was matched by the emergence of truly competitive elections in the USSR for the first time since November 1917. In 1989 a whole new political system was born, with a new independent parliament (the Congress of People's Deputies), a constitution and alternative political groupings. The monopoly of the Communist Party was formally ended in February 1990. Internationally Gorbachev brought about a series of daring policy initiatives to reduce tension. Arms cuts were followed by further arms cuts. The states of Eastern Europe were allowed to 'do it their way' as Gorbachev invoked the Sinatra doctrine to replace the Brezhnev doctrine of limited sovereignty. Gorbachev's approach to foreign affairs was based on what he termed 'new political thinking', which emphasized dialogue, cooperation and peaceful resolution of conflicts. Soviet troops were withdrawn from Afghanistan in 1989. One of the motivations behind this policy was to ease the strain on the ailing Soviet economy.

Rather ironically the problems for Gorbachev were caused by the fact that some of his policies worked too well, and some didn't work at all; in fact they made matters a whole lot worse. The policies of *glasnost* and *democratization* were a resounding success, leading to the growth of pluralism, a revitalization of the media and of the political system and the recovery of society's voice, memory and confidence. This produced a torrent of pent-up grievances, criticism and proposals for change. This became dangerous for the CPSU and Gorbachev because it happened against the background of burgeoning national protest and economic collapse. Gorbachev's economic policies were profoundly unsuccessful. He had managed to dismantle the old economic system of central planning and state ownership quite successfully. Unfortunately, he had nothing to put in its place. Economic conditions declined very rapidly, at the same time as the people were given the chance to speak out and to vote. The Communist Party began to come under fire.

This was exacerbated by the multinational make-up of the USSR. Nationalism provided a language of protest against Soviet rule, and one which was almost impossible to appease in a situation of declining economic fortunes. As the central pillars of the system – the CPSU, Marxist–Leninist ideology, the command economy – began to unravel and lose their credibility, so the ability of the centre to hold the system together in the face of societal protest and movements for separatism and national autonomy was deeply compromised. The only resort that Gorbachev had was to try to rally the progressive forces around himself and hope to buy some time until the economic reforms – radical marketization introduced in the autumn of 1990 – could bear fruit. In the spring of 1990 he created the position of Executive President (with a vast array of powers). He had himself appointed to this position, a massive mistake in hindsight as Gorbachev appeared to lack democratic credibility. The absence of democratic credentials in the Gorbachev Presidency was highlighted starkly by the rise of Boris Yeltsin, Gorbachev's political rival who was popularly elected as the President of Russia in 1990.

Mikhail Sergeevich Gorbachev

He was born on 2 March 1931 in Privolnoye near Stavropol in southern Russia. His mother – an orthodox believer – had him baptized at an early age. His early years were very traumatic. There was a famine in the Stavropol region. Both grandfathers were caught up in the Stalinist terror (one was exiled and one was arrested and tortured). The region was also occupied by the Nazis.

After the war Gorbachev was awarded the Order of the Red Banner of Labour for his exemplary work in 1948, when his brigade brought in 5–6 times more than the average harvest. This, along with his excellent school record (he received a silver medal for his school performance), was enough to earn him a place to study Law at Moscow University in 1950.

At University he met Raisa Titorenko and they married in 1953. He joined the Communist Party in 1952 and also struck up a lifelong friendship with Zdenek Mlynar, a Czech student. He graduated with distinction in 1955 and returned to Stavropol, where he gradually made his way up the hierarchy until in April 1970 he was elected First Secretary of the Stavropol Territory. In 1970 he was elected member of the CPSU Central Committee. In November 1978 he became a Central Committee Secretary for agriculture and moved to Moscow. In 1980 he joined the Politburo.

In March 1985, after three General Secretaries in a row passed away in three years, Gorbachev was elected General Secretary. He introduced a series of radical reforms at home. His initiatives in foreign relations helped to defuse East–West tension and bring an end to the Cold War. He was awarded the Nobel Peace Prize in 1990. At home he proved adept at dismantling the system, but not putting anything in its place, and he was temporarily unseated in a coup in August 1991, before finally resigning as President of the USSR on 25 December 1991 when the USSR ceased to exist.

He ran (unsuccessfully) in the 1996 Russian Presidential Election. He has set up a Foundation to promote democracy, and is head of the Green Cross International, an environmental organization. He has written extensively since leaving office. He was deeply affected by the death of his wife Raisa Gorbachev, who died on 20 September 1999, after a battle with leukemia. She was buried at Novodevichy cemetery in Moscow.

By the middle of 1991, the Soviet system was rapidly polarizing and falling apart. The old guard attempted a botched seizure of power in August 1991, but it was the last hurrah of a discredited group. It failed miserably and with it the CPSU was disbanded (Gorbachev, 1991). A few months later the USSR died on 25 December 1991.

Conclusion

The demise of the Soviet system and the communist idea in Soviet discourse was almost coincidental. In the end the Soviet system could find few to defend it because no one believed in it any more. As soon as the regime set its face to maintain and sustain an existing set of institutions and practices, rather than embracing the need to transform them in line with its stated ideological aims, it ran into trouble. It is difficult to say which was cause, and which effect. Did the decline in belief follow from the declining performance of the system which undermined the ideology's claims about the world and the direction in which it was moving? Or did the decline in belief cause the slowdown and decay by undermining people's belief in and commitment to work for the cause? The Stalinist model – designed as a crash modernization programme – became ossified and almost imposs- ible to dislodge. As the global economy became more advanced, technological and flexible, the Soviet command economy became increasingly anachronistic and dysfunctional.

The declining economic and international power of the USSR was clearly central to the collapse of the communist model. Yet at the heart of the collapse of communism in the USSR was the failure of the Soviet state to convince the Soviet people that it could and should achieve the goals it proclaimed. The dream of creating a society of freedom, equality, liberation and hope fizzled out in a whimper. There were few mourners.

Recommended reading

Useful overviews of the post-Stalin era can be found in: G. Hosking, *A History of the Soviet Union* (Fontana, 1994); C. Read, *The Making and Breaking of the Soviet System* (Palgrave, 2001); M. Sandle, *A Short History of Soviet Socialism* (UCL Press, 1999); A. Nove, *An Economic History of the USSR* (Penguin, 1992); J. Keep, *Last of the Empires* (OUP, 1995).

The best works on Khrushchev are as follows: W. Taubman, *Khrushchev: The Man and His Era* (Norton, 2002); W. Tompson, *Khrushchev: A Political Life* (Macmillan, 1995); D. Filtzer, *The Khrushchev Era: De-Stalinisation and the Limits of Reform* (Macmillan, 1993); N. Khrushchev, *Khrushchev Remembers* (Little Brown, 1971). For Brezhnev, see E. Bacon and M. Sandle (eds), *Brezhnev Reconsidered* (Palgrave, 2002). On foreign policy, see C. Kennedy-Pipe, *Russia and the World 1917–91* (Arnold, 1998). On dissent, see R.L. Tokes (ed.), *Dissent in the USSR* (Johns Hopkins University Press, 1975). On Gorbachev, see R. Sakwa, *Gorbachev and His Reforms* (Routledge, 1990); R. Walker, *Six Years that Shook the World* (MUP, 1993); M. Galeotti, *Gorbachev and His Revolution* (Macmillan, 1995); A. Brown, *The Gorbachev Factor* (Oxford University Press, 1996); M. Gorbachev, *Memoirs* (Doubleday, 1996).

CHAPTER 5

The rise and fall of global communism

Introduction

THE USSR PROCLAIMED it was embarking on a mission to make the whole world communist. After defeating the fascist threat in the Great Patriotic War 1941–45, the world gradually began to turn Red. Starting in Eastern Europe after 1945, states in Asia, Africa, the Caribbean and Latin America joined the communist bloc and took sides in the global conflict between capitalism and communism. Initially, the new communist states accepted the leadership and hegemony of the USSR. They modelled themselves very closely on the pattern of economic transformation, social structure and political leadership adopted in the USSR, and received substantial amounts of aid and resources from the USSR. Inexorably though, differences began to emerge, as each state developed a distinctive national interpretation of the Soviet model of communist theory and practice. Although it was common to talk of the Soviet bloc in monolithic terms, as the decades progressed it became clear that there were a number of different 'communisms' in existence. Although all communists in this period declared themselves to be faithful disciples of Marxism–Leninism, committed to the realization of Marx's ultimate vision of a communist society, they did not agree entirely on the best way to get there, or how quickly to go. In this chapter we will examine briefly the different forms that communism took, and examine the rapid decline of communism in the late 1980s and 1990s. Let us begin close to the communist 'home': Eastern Europe.

'Communisms' in Eastern Europe

Why did the states of Eastern Europe turn communist after 1945? The simple answer – because Stalin wanted it – is tempting but deceptive. Clearly Stalin did want it. But *why* did he want it? Was he hell-bent on global domination for communism, and this was the first step in achieving this aim? Or was he motivated by security concerns after the horrors of the Nazi invasion and occupation? Did he want it because circumstances and international considerations – the wheeling and dealing with Churchill and Roosevelt – had given him a window of opportunity which was just too good to miss? Unearthing his motivations is not easy. But Stalin wasn't the only person who wanted it. Any explanation of the reasons for the communist takeover needs to take into account the actions and aspirations of local communist leaders, the non-communist political groups and the people of the states of Eastern Europe too (Okey, 1982; Fowkes, 1993).

The victories of the Red Army over the retreating German forces after 1944 in Eastern Europe posed some difficult issues for Stalin who was keen to secure control over the region, as a minimum to enhance Soviet security and as a maximum to provide the platform for further expansion. But this was not something solely dictated from Moscow. Communist groups across this region had participated in the resistance movement and were pushing for a share of power. Indeed, the communists alone seemed to have the political cohesion to survive in the period after 1945. The populations of Eastern Europe appear to have been at best indifferent to capitalism, being in a region of impoverishment and ethnic tensions (although they were by no means enthusiastic about communism either). The whole experience of Nazi occupation and Red Army 'liberation' had been deeply traumatic for the peoples of Eastern Europe. In this situation, the communists appeared with a message of hope: society could be reconstructed and rebuilt afresh.

Stalin wanted to control the region. The local communists wished to assume power and, having achieved power, to implement the Stalinist model. The interventions of the Red Army provided the opportunity to send politically trained agents and 'experts' from Moscow to assist the local communists. But it is important also to note two things. First, that in countries whose victory over the Germans owed little to the Red Army – Yugoslavia and Albania – communists still came to power (and might well have done in Greece as well). Second, Stalin was initially wary of a too hasty transition to communism, and so at times he attempted to slow down those communists he did not directly control, and also to tone down the actions and rhetoric of those he did. For instance, Stalin responded to the pressure from the West to broaden the governments in Romania and Poland with members of the traditional political parties. Stalin's overall intentions are still rather murky. At times he appeared to be working incrementally, pragmatically, gradually according to the demands of the local and international environment. At others, there appeared to be a master plan unfolding, the so-called salami tactics outlined by Matyas Rakosi: communism would advance across Eastern Europe, slice by slice (Fowkes, 1993: 6–51; Okey, 1982: 188–98).

Apart from Yugoslavia (under Josip Tito) and Albania (under Enver Hoxha) who both maintained an independent line, most of the countries which were to comprise the Soviet bloc – Poland, Czechoslovakia, Hungary, Bulgaria, Romania, East Germany – came under the hegemony of Moscow. This was entirely predictable given the USSR's place as the first socialist state, as the state which had defeated the Nazis, and given that most communist leaders recognized that not only was it the USSR/Red Army which could put them into power, but also it was likely that the USSR would be needed to maintain them in power and help rebuild their war-ravaged economies. However, the emergence of communist regimes was not a uniform process. The method and pace of the communist takeovers in Eastern Europe varied from country to country, although a basic pattern can be detected, which suggests some orchestration from Moscow. The takeovers began in 1945/46 and were completed by 1948.

In the initial stages, the communists would participate in some kind of Popular Front coalition, which had as its aim the relatively neutral goal of reconstructing the country with little ideological dogma in the solutions put forward. At a later stage, the communists began to move away from a coalition-based approach, and their agents began to take over the key ministries of defence, security and the secret police. Rival groups were marginalized, divided and removed. By February 1948 a mass resignation of non-communist ministers provoked a political crisis in Czechoslovakia which culminated in the victory of Gottwald and the communists. Eastern Europe was now communist. But Eastern Europe was not wholly dominated from Moscow (Stern, 1990: 98–99).

Stalinization and Sovietization

After 1948, the communist countries in Eastern Europe began to formally pattern themselves on the Soviet model. The exceptions to this, as we have seen, were the states of Yugoslavia and Albania. In the immediate aftermath of the Second World War, Tito had been a staunch critic of the West and a fervent admirer of socialism Soviet-style. Yugoslavia appeared, on the surface, to be the most loyal member of the newly emerging socialist bloc in Eastern Europe. Appearances were deceptive though. Tito's communists had won power through the sacrifices of their own struggle and were unwilling to compromise this independence once in power. Stalin was suspicious of independently minded local communist leaders. Relations quickly deteriorated after 1946. Stalin wanted to exploit the reserves of Eastern Europe to fund the repair of the Soviet economy back home, whereas Tito wanted assistance from the USSR in reconstructing his own economy. The straw that broke the camel's back though was Tito's plan for a Balkan Federation – including Yugoslavia, Bulgaria, Albania and possibly Greece (if a successful communist takeover could be 'arranged') – which Stalin baulked at. It seemed, from Moscow's perspective, that Tito was trying to organize an alternative communist power bloc. Stalin responded to this by organizing for Yugoslavia to be ejected from Cominform. Cominform (the Communist Information Bureau) was created in September 1947, to coordinate actions between communist parties, under Moscow direction. The expulsion of Yugoslavia on 28 June 1948 was a seminal moment in the history of communism in Eastern Europe: the persistence of Tito's regime demonstrated that it was possible to take a different, non-Soviet road to socialism and communism (Stern, 1990: 106–19).

The repercussions of this action were only to be felt later on, as a distinctive Titoist approach to the building of socialism began to emerge. In place of the Soviet model of building socialism and communism based on collectivization, industrialization and central planning, the Yugoslavs developed a more decentralized model, giving much greater powers to the six republics, and instituted a socialist market economy. In effect Tito had created a 'national' road to socialism. This development was mirrored in Albania where Enver Hoxha adopted a similarly independent stance. Adhering staunchly to the Stalinist line, Hoxha broke with Yugoslavia in 1948 and refused to support the denunciation of Stalin made by Khrushchev in 1956. Isolated in Eastern Europe, in 1960 Hoxha turned for support to Beijing after the Sino-Soviet split, and Albania remained shut off from the rest of Europe until Hoxha's death in 1985. Together, these two Balkan states planted the seeds for the demise of communism in Eastern Europe. Just as Stalin was attempting to create a more or less monolithic Soviet bloc in Eastern Europe directed from Moscow, so Tito and Hoxha had proven that a national version of communism was possible. This nationalist seed was to grow and grow after 1953, culminating in the cataclysmic events of 1989.

For the rest of Eastern Europe, the period between 1948 and 1953 witnessed a period of Stalinization, as the Stalinist model was uniformly applied. Uniform constitutions were imposed, creating a political system with a democratic appearance (e.g. sovereign national assemblies), but in reality these were mere fronts for the rule of the local Politburo. Stalinist political practices were accompanied by Stalinist economic practices: central planning, 5-year plans and a focus on heavy industry. Economic control of Eastern Europe was coordinated through COMECON (the Council for Mutual Economic Assistance) which was set up in 1949 in response to the Marshall Plan in order to keep Eastern Europe free of western interference and to ensure that the economic activities of these states gave priority to the interests of the USSR. In the agricultural sector each of the states undertook the drive to collectivize agriculture, although this was a much more fraught and gradual process, given the numerical preponderance of peasants in the economies of much of Eastern Europe. By 1953, the process of Sovietizing/Stalinizing Eastern Europe, of recreating the Soviet bloc in the USSR's image, was well under way (Fowkes, 1993: 52–75; Kaser, 1967). The death of Stalin in 1953 was to herald a period of great change.

Communism in Eastern Europe: de-Stalinization and polycentrism

The shock waves of Stalin's death were felt as far away as Belgrade and Beijing. The end of the Stalinist dictatorship in the USSR forced a search for a mechanism of control among communists in Eastern Europe that was not based around terror, purges, censorship and personal dictatorship. The result was the emergence of a number of movements for reform and autonomy in Eastern Europe, as national roads to communism began to be built. Far from being a monolithic bloc of states, Eastern Europe in this period witnessed the rise of polycentrism in the Soviet bloc. Throughout the period from 1953 to 1989 there were revolts by workers in East Germany in 1953, and protests in Hungary and Poland in 1956, in Czechoslovakia in 1968, and Poland in 1970, 1976 and 1980 (Fowkes, 1993; Crampton, 1994).

The death of Stalin provoked a fierce power struggle in the Kremlin, as well as a series of reforms in the USSR, and these ripples were felt in Eastern Europe. The contest between Khrushchev, Malenkov and Molotov had repercussions for the relations between Moscow and Eastern Europe, as each leader developed their own particular policy stance. The reforms in the USSR – moves towards collective leadership, greater concern for the living standards of the population, a cultural 'thaw' and the need to bring about party control of the secret police and to reduce the reliance on terror as a means of governance – seemed to herald a new climate of greater liberalization. Yet in Eastern Europe the local leaders (the 'little Stalins', like Ulbricht and Rakosi) all seemed reluctant to follow suit. Having been appointed by Stalin, and undertaken, with varying degrees of vigour, a purge of their opponents, these 'little Stalins' now realized the future was a good deal more uncertain. This sense of uncertainty was magnified by events in 1955. Khrushchev agreed to withdraw Soviet troops from Austria, but at the same time he created the Warsaw Pact on 14 May 1955, a communist equivalent to NATO (involving a military friendship treaty, a counterpart to COMECON). At the end of May 1955, however, Khrushchev decided it was time for a thawing in relations with

Yugoslavia, and he went to Belgrade and publicly embraced Tito. The messages Khrushchev sent out with these two events in May 1955 were a little bit mixed, to say the least. The Warsaw Pact – a unified military under Soviet command – implied the subordination of defence/security interests to an organization run from Moscow. The rapprochement with Tito seemed to legitimize political pluralism in Eastern Europe, national roads to communism and different types of communism from the Moscow 'flavour'. On the one hand, the Warsaw Pact seemed to imply limits on Eastern European autonomy. On the other, it seemed to be suggesting that Moscow would actively tolerate more expressions of autonomy. This ambiguity created tensions which were to surface periodically in Eastern Europe between 1956 and 1989 (Stern, 1990: ch. 8).

Although there had already been some protests in East Germany and Czechoslovakia in 1953, it was Khrushchev's 'secret speech' in February 1956 which was to spark a series of upheavals as Hungary, Poland and Czechoslovakia all sought to develop a national brand of communism. Khrushchev's speech reverberated around the capitals of Eastern Europe, leading many to question the nature of the system put in place under Stalin. Reforms and change were now on the agenda. But how much change would Moscow allow? In Poland in 1956, the Soviets were prepared to allow some reforms so long as the party retained sole control, and Poland remained fully aligned to the Warsaw Pact: hence the negotiations of October 1956 which precluded interventions from Soviet tanks. Budapest was not so lucky. Concerns in Moscow that Hungary was going to secede from the Soviet bloc amid mass demonstrations and protests on the street led to armed intervention. Khrushchev sent in the tanks to crush the uprising. Many thousands died or fled. Twelve years later in Prague, a reform movement to install 'socialism with a human face' was dealt with similarly brutally by Brezhnev who sent the tanks in to crush the movement led by the reform communist Alexander Dubcek. Military units from the USSR, Bulgaria, Hungary, Poland and East Germany all participated in this invasion. This ushered in the 'Brezhnev doctrine' of limited sovereignty for the states of Eastern Europe (Fowkes, 1993: chs 5 & 7; Crampton, 1994: chs 16–18).

Overall, between 1956 and 1985, the Soviets were willing to tolerate a degree of departure from the Soviet model. Most states undertook economic reforms – including decentralization, experiments with marketization, changes to the operation of the agricultural sphere – but the Soviets were unwilling to tolerate anything which could endanger the political or military hegemony of the USSR. The only states which departed from the Soviet script were Yugoslavia (as we saw earlier) and also Romania under the hardline Ceausescu. Even then Romania remained resolutely neo-Stalinist at home. Her 'dissidence' was a tendency to display certain maverick foreign policy tendencies, most notably with regard to policies towards China and Israel (Stern, 1990: 201–02). In sum, throughout the period from 1956 to 1980, the Soviet pattern of communist development remained. The states of Eastern Europe continued their gradual transformation into modern, urban civilizations. Protest and conflict began to die down. The region appeared relatively stable. It wasn't until 1980 and the strikes and protests led by ship workers in Gdansk, Poland, that the surface calm was disturbed, revealing what lay beneath. Nine years later the entire rickety edifice was to come tumbling down in a matter of months, as the seeds of nationalism finally blossomed. Before we explore the momentous events of 1989, let us look briefly at communism elsewhere across the globe, starting with the experience of the Chinese communists.

Red Star in the East: China and Asian communism

The main challenge to Soviet hegemony – ideological, political, economic and international – from within the bloc of communist countries came from China. The Chinese Communist Party came to power in 1949 after a protracted struggle against both the Japanese and the Chinese nationalists (Kuomintang). Although initially they held very closely to the Soviet model and to Soviet ideological and political leadership, from 1955/56 onwards the CCP began to move away from the Soviet approach and developed their own interpretation of communism and their own policy imperatives, under the leadership of Chou En-Lai and Mao Zedong (Blecher, 1986; Saich, 1981; Schram, 1974; Dirlik, 1989).

Mao Zedong

He was born on 26 December 1893, to a moderately well-to-do peasant in Hunan province.

Mao did not leave his village until the age of 17 when he went to middle school in Changsha, the capital of Hunan. That year, 1911, the revolution led by Dr Sun Yat-Sen overthrew the imperial government and Mao became caught up in the political instability. He left his studies at the school and after a period in a revolutionary army he began to study at a Hunan provincial library on his own. He became well acquainted with the works of Darwin, Mill and Rousseau before he ran out of money and joined a teaching course.

Instead of becoming a teacher at the completion of his course in 1918 he went to Beijing and became a poorly paid assistant in the university library. There he found two allies, the library chief Li Ta-chao, and a professor of literature, Chen Tu-hsui, who were radical Marxists and later founded the Chinese Communist Party, the CCP. While in Beijing he married his first wife, Yang Kaihui.

In 1923 he was elected to the Central Committee of the CCP at its Third Congress. As the Civil War in China began to extend, Mao moved into the Jinggang mountains and established a Chinese Soviet republic, where he experimented with rural reforms and forms of mobile warfare. Under intense pressure from the nationalist Kuomintang, the Communists – led by Mao – undertook the 'Long March' (about 9,600 km) to the north-west of China.

There Mao led communist resistance to the Japanese invasion and eventually defeated the nationalist forces led by Chiang Kai-Shek, establishing the People's Republic of China on 1 October 1949. Between 1949 and 1960, Mao oversaw a rapid transformation of the Chinese economy (at a very great human cost) as well as a rapid consolidation of his own power. Mao also broke with the USSR and sought hegemony for China in the socialist bloc. A Mao cult began to grow up. In October 1966 the *Quotations from Chairman Mao Zedong* (also known as the 'Little Red Book') was published. Party members were encouraged to carry a copy with them everywhere they went. Mao's image became increasingly prominent in Chinese public life.

In 1966, Mao unleashed the devastating Cultural Revolution on the Chinese people. Ten years later Mao died aged 83 on 9 September 1976, from either Parkinson's disease or motor neuron disease.

When the CCP came to power in October 1949 after a prolonged and bitter campaign, the country was in tatters. Devastated by war, civil war, the legacy of imperialism and internal conflicts, China was facing economic ruin and social collapse. The similarities with the Bolshevik seizure of power and the situation facing Lenin *et al.* are quite striking, emphasizing perhaps the importance of a 'crisis' of some kind and the collapse of state power for a successful communist revolution to occur. However, unlike the Bolsheviks, the CCP started more gradually on the road to communism, and this started them on a path which proved to be very distinct from that of their Soviet neighbour. The first steps between 1949 and 1952 were concerned with reconstruction and recovery in the economic field, and the elimination of opposition in the political field. Underpinning this approach was the desire to lay the foundations for subsequent development and also to try to garner as much support as possible from the Chinese people for the new regime. Hence the choice of name for the new state: *The People's Republic of China*, playing on the patriotism of the masses. The recovery ethos meant moderate reforms to benefit the workers and peasants (but also some capitalist elements). A wide-ranging land reform was introduced which dispossessed the landlords and redistributed the land to the peasantry. Nationalization of industry proceeded slowly, and the CCP tolerated the continued existence of many small businesses as part of the broad coalition approach to governing and as a way of promoting the speediest possible recovery. Wide-ranging social reforms – including measures to outlaw infanticide, crack down on pimps and drug dealers, and to upgrade the position of women in Chinese society – were all enacted. By the end of 1952, the recovery of the economy was almost complete (Blecher, 1986: 42–53). What developmental strategy would the CCP pursue?

The initial strategy was categorized by Mao as 'leaning to one side' and meant learning from the experience of the USSR. The conscious aping of the Soviet model meant importing particular patterns and practices which ran against the grain of indigenous

Chinese development. The emphasis on the urban sector, as opposed to the rural roots and priorities of Chinese communism, the focus on heavy industry not agriculture, the excessive centralization of the economy were all applied in China after 1952 as, with a great fanfare, the first 5-year plan was announced in 1953 as the start of the 'general programme for the transition to socialism'. The decision to adopt the Soviet pattern was fairly straightforward: it appeared to be working very successfully in the USSR and was being exported into Eastern Europe. China, like Eastern Europe, needed Soviet aid, technical assistance and technology if it was to undertake the building of socialism and communism. The 'Soviet imitation' period did not last very long though (Blecher, 1986: 53–68). Why?

Although the Soviet period did produce successful economic results in the industrial sector, agricultural production lagged behind, and it appeared that the party was sacrificing the interests of the peasantry for the benefit of the heavy industrial sector. The development of the rural areas was stifled and the gap between town and country was growing. These economic difficulties began to raise doubts in the minds of the Chinese leadership. These doubts were exacerbated by Khrushchev's denunciation of Stalin in 1956. This was a difficult time for Mao, as the same accusations – of accruing excessive personal power to himself – could have been levelled at him. Initially, the CCP cautiously welcomed the openly self-critical attitude of the CPSU towards its past. However, when the events began to unfold in Hungary, Mao began to take a different tack. Mao was unwilling to accept many of the criticisms of Stalin, and believed that the dangers inherent in anti-Stalinism (a species of that terrible crime 'revisionism') could be seen by looking at events in Hungary. Mao drew two conclusions from what happened in Budapest. First, that there were dangers in just slavishly copying the Soviet model. Second, that revisionism/anti-Stalinism could create dangerous tensions and should be combated. In December 1956, Mao's line was published in the Chinese press. This lead article outlined that the USSR was the 'centre' of the international communist movement (not the leader), and refused to acknowledge that the Soviet leadership had the sole claim to interpret Marxism–Leninism. Mao also warned against excessive criticism of Stalin (Stern, 1990: chs 7 & 10).

The stage was set for a collision course between the two major socialist states. The CCP began, under Mao's leadership, to develop a distinctive model of socialism which differed greatly from the Soviet pattern. The implications of the events of 1956 and 1957 were enormous for the international communist movement. China was not only creating an alternative way to build socialism and communism, but it was also starting to criticize the USSR on the grounds of its ideological purity and credibility. This was now a frontal challenge to Soviet hegemony. China could not be invaded and crushed like Hungary. China could not be isolated and marginalized like Yugoslavia. The CCP had the potential to create an alternative socialist bloc, and to undermine the global domination of the USSR. The fragmentation of the communist world was spreading.

The Great Leap Forward to the Cultural Revolution 1957–66

The CCP wanted to reach the same goal as the Soviets. The divergence came over how to get there. This transition between the 'here and now' and the 'not yet' was to become a matter of bitter doctrinal dispute and political wrangling, as each communist party asserted its claim to be the authentic, true interpreter of the writings of Marx and Engels. The emergence of an alternative Chinese model came in 1957 with the implementation of Mao's policy of the 'Great Leap Forward'. Increasingly disgruntled by the policy of Sovietization, Mao decided it was time to make a break and so he formulated a new approach in 1958. This one would restore traditional Chinese priorities and rely on the one resource China had in abundance: labour power. The Great Leap Forward (GLF), as it became known, was based on:

- a more balanced strategy of economic development, rather than an emphasis upon heavy industry;

- economic growth that was fuelled by intensive exploitation of labour, rather than through capital intensive methods;

- central planning that yielded to a more decentralized approach (Blecher, 1986: 68–80).

In the countryside, the GLF was realized through the creation of what became known as *People's Communes*, which combined agricultural and industrial production and synthesized political, social and economic tasks in one unit. Each commune (which comprised initially about 5,000 homes) would share all things equally, and all members would give their labour freely. In their most radical incarnation, these communes seemed to embody the values of Marxist communism: radically egalitarian and collectivist. Mao was acutely aware of the ideological potential in the communes, and the CCP claimed that they signified that China had made considerable strides towards the construction of

communism. Coming at the same time as Khrushchev was for-
mulating his Third Party Programme, the Chinese claims were a
forthright frontal challenge to the USSR's position as the most
advanced socialist state. Khrushchev belittled the Chinese declara-
tions in 1959, arguing that it was not possible to go directly
from capitalism to communism, and that they had 'a poor idea of
what communism is and how it is to be built' (Stern, 1990: 179).
It is only against this international background that we can make
full sense of the boldness of Khrushchev proclaiming that communism would be built 'in the main' by 1980. Khrushchev was a
leader in a hurry.

The Great Leap Forward met with mixed economic success
in its first couple of years. It seemed to be on course to meet its
targets, but in 1959 and 1960 problems multiplied. Production
levels fell and, accompanied by floods and droughts, this led to
food shortages and devastating famines. From 1959 onwards, an
economic policy reorientation began. Before the new policy line
could be established, the schism between Moscow and Beijing
became a formal split. The simmering tensions that had been
growing more acute since the mid-1950s – over international
policy, economic priorities, ideological differences, personality
clashes, and long-standing great power rivalries – broke out
into open hostility in 1960. The Chinese attacked Khrushchev's
'revisionism', arguing that the parliamentary road to socialism
was an illusion and that all support had to be given to national-
liberation struggles in the Third World. The Soviets refuted this,
arguing that there were many roads to socialism and that not
all revolutionary struggles should be supported, as they could
prove counter-productive. The best way to ensure the victory of
communism was to support the rapid development of the Soviet

economy. The crucial moment came when the Soviets decided to withdraw all technicians and aid. At the 1960 Moscow Conference of International Communist parties, the Chinese began to court support, drawing North Korea, North Vietnam and Albania into their orbit. The split became irrevocable in 1962 during the Cuban Missile Crisis. The two parties continued to snipe at each other throughout the 1960s, 1970s and early 1980s. It wasn't until the advent of Gorbachev that the 'Communist Cold War' began to thaw.

Chinese communism 1966–89

Chinese communism underwent a major evolution after 1960. The radical revolutionary energy in the Cultural Revolution of 1966 gave way to the economic reforms of the 1970s and 1980s which laid the basis for the transformation of China in the twenty-first century into one of the leading capitalist economies (albeit overseen by a communist party!) in the world. In the Cultural Revolution, Mao unleashed a torrent of criticism, destruction and unconstrained violence from students and other radical groups who formed themselves into 'Red Guards'. Their aim was to try to restore the revolutionary fervour and ideals of the system by attacking all the centres of authority: bureaucrats, experts, intellectuals and so on. Books were destroyed. Writers and other intellectuals were forced into terrible public humiliations. 'Permanent revolution' was supposed to give real power and control to the people. It soon spiralled out of control, sweeping thousands upon thousands of people up in the flood of chaos. It wasn't until 1969 that some kind of stability was created, although it dragged on fitfully until Mao's death in 1976 (Brugger, 1978).

His death led to a prolonged struggle, in terms of both the succession and also the economic direction of the state. After 1979, the Chinese began to implement a series of economic reforms which aimed to import western technologies, use limited privatization and economic deregulation and achieve western living standards. The radical egalitarianism and absolute collectivism of the *People's Communes* of the 1950s had been abandoned.

Was Chinese communism distinct from the Soviet version? Although both communist states shared a common goal, they took different roads in their attempts to get there, and both ended up by abandoning their ostensible goal, although in China the communists remain (for the present) in power. Although the CCP did consciously import and adopt Stalinist industrialization techniques and practices, even these were quite clearly *sinified*, taking far greater account of the needs of the peasantry than in the USSR. After 1957 though, the Chinese adopted a very different approach to the building of socialism and communism in the socio-economic sphere. The monopoly of power of the CCP remained unchallenged. The Maoist approach entailed radical, mass mobilization of labour and the active fostering of local collectivism, self-reliance, anti-elitism and anti-bureaucratism. This gave way after his death to a strategy of limited privatization, individual entrepreneurship and more stable political arrangements. Mao in many ways overturned the fundamental tenets of Marxism: peasants, not workers, as the main revolutionary group; the Third World, not Europe, as the locus of the revolutionary struggle (Pipes, 2002: 130–32). In essence, while the Soviets tried minor variations on a similar theme between 1953 and 1985, the Chinese lurched from radical 'leftist' to cautious 'rightist' programmes as they sought a path to socialism and modernity.

Communism in Asia: nationalism, communism and anti-colonialism

Communism refused to stay within the confines of China. The movements for national liberation in South-East Asia and the globalization of the Cold War saw the emergence of communist regimes across Asia. The revolt against colonial rule produced a fusion of nationalism and communism in states like Korea, Vietnam, Kampuchea, Mongolia and Laos. The pattern of revolution was often based upon a loose application of the Chinese or Maoist model: establishing footholds in the countryside, espousing the interests of the nation as a whole, using civil war as part of the revolutionary struggle and maintaining close links between the party and the masses. However, a pattern similar to the one in Eastern Europe can be detected among the Asian communist states. After starting off following the Soviet/Chinese model and espousing loyalty to the teachings of Marxism–Leninism, gradually, inexorably the *national* displaced the *communist*, until little that could be identified as authentically communist was left. Let us look at one or two examples.

The partitioning of Korea after 1945 led to the establishment of the Democratic People's Republic of Korea in 1948 (in the north) and the Republic of Korea (in the south). The communists in the north were led by Kim Il Sung (who had fought with the Chinese in their struggle for power) and the Korean Workers' Party. After a bitter conflict with the south caused by Kim's surprise invasion, the KWP implemented a Stalinist model of development. Kim began to lean towards Beijing rather than Moscow during the 1960s, and eventually adopted a stance of neutrality in the 1970s. Gradually, North Korea under Kim Il Sung developed an isolationist, autarkic mentality. The dominant ideological framework of North Korean communism was *juche* rather than Marxism–Leninism: emphasizing independence, self-reliance, self-defence. Kim developed an increasingly outlandish personality cult and established a highly centralized, regimented, militarized and indoctrinated society. The economy hit a crisis in the 1970s and has been in trouble ever since, with living standards declining for the mass of the people. Kim also turned North Korea into a family dynasty, being succeeded by his son Kim Jong-Il in 1994 (Stern, 1990: 128–32).

Communism in Vietnam, Laos and Cambodia came about as a result of the national-liberation struggle against the occupying imperialist powers. The Vietnamese communist regime was born in 1954 after the partition of the country at the Geneva Conference. Under the leadership of Ho Chi Minh, the Vietnamese communists undertook a prolonged struggle against the USA and the South Vietnamese, until unification in 1976 and the creation of the Socialist Republic of Vietnam. Since 1986, the Vietnamese communists, in line with developments in China, have undertaken a series of economic reforms – lifting restrictions on private enterprise, opening a stock exchange, normalizing trade relations with the capitalist powers – which have eroded the traditional communist practices of nationalization and central planning. However, single-party domination, censorship and controls on dissent continue to operate (Beresford, 1988). Similarly, the communist regime which was installed in Laos in December 1975 was heavily dependent upon Soviet aid and assistance as it implemented a highly centralized economic mechanism and draconian political and social policies aimed at stamping out dissent.

The most extreme example of communism in South-East Asia came in Kampuchea (Ponchaud, 1978; Jackson, 1989). The regime of Pol Pot and the Khmer Rouge was a most callous, brutal and murderous one. They came to power on the back of the opposition to the terrible destruction wrought by the US bombing campaign on the Ho Chi Minh trail, seizing control of the capital Phnom Penh in 1975. They ruled for four years until 1979, in which time many Cambodians lost their lives owing to starvation, execution or brutal work conditions. Pol Pot took Mao's approach – pro-peasant, ruthless, amoral, bent on writing new identities on all Kampuchean people by obliterating their former way of life. The Khmer Rouge undertook a series of cataclysmic policies which turned the whole country upside down. The first indication of the radical changes to come was the declaration that the seizure of power marked the onset of 'Year Zero'. Nothing before this time mattered, and so the party set about a total remake of people and society. They undertook a rapid radical de-urbanization believing that the cities were sources of decay and evil. All opposition, or potential opposition, was destroyed. Intellectuals, monks, teachers, students, civil servants (and their families) were executed or sent to the 'killing fields'. Books were destroyed. Money was burnt. Schools were shut down. Like in Rwanda, or the holocaust in Nazi Germany, the suffering endured is almost too horrific to describe. In the countryside, the Khmer Rouge organized the people into rural co-operatives which were set up on the basis of the People's Communes created by Mao during the era of the GLF. They were radically egalitarian in their outlook: a communal kitchen, dormitories separated along gender lines, and food appropriated by the state. The invasion of Kampuchea by the Vietnamese in 1979 led to the eventual downfall of Pol Pot and the Khmer Rouge.

Cuba, Latin America, Africa

Outside Eastern Europe, China and South-East Asia, the most well-known communist state is Cuba under the leadership of Fidel Castro (Horowitz, 1989). However, Cuba was not the only communist state in Latin America. There was a short-lived communist government in Chile between 1970–73 led by Salvador Allende. The Allende interlude is an interesting example, because the communists came to power via the ballot box, not by revolution or force of arms. Allende headed a coalition of socialists, communists, social democrats and dissident Christian Democrats under the banner of 'Popular Unity'. Having emerged victorious, Allende embarked on a programme of radical social transformation. The state oversaw the expropriation of vast amounts of land and its distribution to the poor peasants as part of the collectivization of the agricultural sector. Allende then proceeded with the nationalization of large parts of the industrial sector (most notably the mineral extraction industries: copper, coal, iron and nitrate) and also the banks. Foreign investment began to plummet and Chile became the recipient of large amounts of Soviet aid. In the end the Allende government was upstaged by a military coup led by Augusto Pinochet, although the economy was in a crisis state and the government had been destabilized by the actions of the CIA. Allende's policies were another variant on the national modernization/communist approach that characterized communist regimes in the Third World, combining nationalization of industry, control of the financial levers, land reform and collective or cooperative agriculture. Where Chile differed from the other examples we have seen lay in the political context. Chile's coalition took and exercised power in a situation of political pluralism, limited by a Constitution and a Supreme Court, with a relatively open and free media (Alexander, 1978).

Fidel Castro

He was born on 13 August 1926 into a wealthy farming family in Holguin Province. He was educated in a variety of religious (Jesuit) and private schools before joining the University of Havana to study law in 1945. There he joined with a revolutionary grouping, the Insurrectional Revolutionary Union. In 1948 he married Mirta Diaz Balart, a philosophy student from a wealthy Cuban family. They had a son Fidelito.

In 1950 he graduated, and began practising law, defending the poor and dispossessed. Castro became embroiled in the political violence of Cuba in the early 1950s and after a short spell in prison (1953–55) he went into exile in Mexico on 7 July. There he established, with other exiles, the 26 July Movement.

After a prolonged struggle with the forces of Fulgencio Batista, Castro's forces entered Havana on 5 January 1959. His nationalist economic policies caused great concern in the USA, especially the nationalization of the sugar industry. Over one million Cubans left Cuba to go to the USA and became vocal critics of Castro.

In April 1961, the USA launched its abortive, unsuccessful Bay of Pigs invasion funded by the CIA. Castro rapidly gravitated towards the USSR as a result of US hostility, and declared himself a Marxist–Leninist in 1962. In the same year, the Cuban Missile Crisis broke which placed Castro at the centre of the world's attention. Over the next 25 years, Cuba played a key role in the Soviet bloc, supporting Soviet policy and providing assistance to Marxist groups in Angola and elsewhere. The withdrawal of Soviet aid in the late 1980s and the collapse of communism in 1991 brought severe difficulties to the Cuban economy. In the early 1990s Castro loosened the restrictions on religion.

While Allende lasted only three years, Fidel Castro in Cuba has proven to be one of the great survivors of twentieth-century politics. Castro came to power in 1959 as part of a nationalist revolt against US influence in Cuba under the dictatorial regime of Fulgencio Batista (whom rather ironically the Cuban communists had supported until this point). Cuba seemed on the surface to be a most unlikely candidate for a communist revolution: relatively affluent (by Latin American standards), the economy was reasonably well developed. Both indigenous communists and the USSR did not consider Castro's seizure of power to be an authentically communist one, merely a national revolt against US colonialism. However, as US opposition mounted, so Castro began to merge his movement with the communists and gradually he was absorbed into the Soviet orbit. The debacle of the attempted US invasion in 1961 and the Cuban Missile Crisis of 1962 all served to push Castro into a very close alliance with Moscow. The Soviets provided an enormous amount of economic and military assistance to the Cubans. Between 1961 and 1965 a series of political deals resulted in the formation of the Cuban Communist Party in October 1965. Once again, the communism which emerged in Cuba was a fusion of nationalism/anti-colonialism, a particular interpretation of Marxism–Leninism and the Soviet pattern of political domination and socio-economic modernization (Horowitz, 1989; Gil, 1969).

The Cuban model rested on a fundamental reshaping of indigenous institutions and practices along the lines of the Soviet model, accompanied by active attempts to start revolutions elsewhere in Latin America. A one-party vanguard state shaped along the same lines as that of the USSR, Cuban communism has been totally dominated by the figure of Fidel Castro who was head of the party, the government and the armed forces. In economic terms, the Cuban Communist Party patterned itself on the Soviet model, centralizing and nationalizing industry (although agriculture remained a mixed sector incorporating private and state farms). The economy up until 1991 was supported by Soviet subsidies. The USSR provided Cuba with oil, and Cuba reciprocated with sugar. The Cubans invested heavily in health care and educational facilities for the population. The Cuban communists have gradually been forced to diversify and open up to greater contact with the capitalist world as the demise of the USSR cut off the supply of subsidies and cheap oil. Tourism has grown rapidly in the 1990s as a key source of income. The radical leftist regime of Hugo Chavez in Venezuela is now one of Cuba's most important trading partners. The persistence of the Cuban Communist Party, rather like the Chinese Communist Party, is testament to the adaptability and flexibility of the party and its ability to meet the needs of its own population and to suppress dissent. This combination of monopolistic political controls alongside a diversification of economic practices and a strongly nationalist orientation has served to maintain Castro and his regime in power. As with all other communist systems since 1945, the idea of building socialism and communism has all but disappeared.

Communism in Africa

In Africa, the rise of communist parties also developed out of the struggle for independence from western colonial rule, carried out against the backdrop of the Cold War, as both the Americans and the Soviet/Chinese blocs attempted to recruit for themselves client states/satellites through aid, military assistance and other levers. But I think it is fair to say that, although certain parties and certain states were quick to adopt particular aspects of the Soviet model and of Marxist–Leninist ideology (most notably the Leninist critique of imperialism and the concept of a one-party vanguard state), there was very little enthusiasm for the project of building Soviet-style communism on African soil (Beller & Rejai, 1969; Stern, 1990: 239–41; Sakwa, 1999). One of the reasons for this is the close intertwining with the struggle for independence from imperialism and capitalism. For many Africans, the goals of Soviet-style communism seemed a bit too similar to those of the capitalist states who had been their oppressors. Leopold Senghor (1906–2001), the President of Senegal from 1960–80, stated that:

[t]he paradox in the building of socialism in communist countries, or at least in the Soviet Union, is that it increasingly resembles capitalistic growth in the USA, the American way of life, with high salaries, refrigerators, washing machines and television sets, but with less art and less freedom of thought. (Beller & Rejai, 1969: 228)

In the struggle for power, African socialists and Marxists showed a degree of unwillingness to commit themselves exclusively to Marxism–Leninism or communism. There was instead a greater willingness to emphasize the fight for national independence. In the post-revolutionary stages, the adoption of Soviet approaches or policies or institutions was usually done as a result of one or more imperatives. First, as a lever for extracting support and assistance from the USSR or China in its programme of nation-building, or for assistance in a conflict (be it internal or external). Secondly, because as a pattern of modernization and nation-building in a situation of scarce resources, the Stalinist model had proven itself successful in the short run. Hence the adoption of policies of nationalization, central planning and collectivization of agriculture. Thirdly, the Leninist model of a single-party state enabled the Marxist parties to centralize power and remove opposition in the sometimes chaotic situation after independence. Communism and communist practices have thus been used in Africa primarily as means of modernization, nation-building and consolidation of power after independence. This is a similar pattern to the one in Asia, whereby the fusion of the struggle for liberation and the struggle for socialism and communism has in the long run turned out to mean that nationalism has displaced communism as the *raison d'être* of the post-colonial regime. The African states which adopted Marxism–Leninism as their official ideology and said that they were in the process of building socialism and communism were: Angola, Mozambique, Madagascar, Congo-Brazzaville, Benin and Ethiopia. Perhaps the best example of an African state most closely committed to Marxism–Leninism and the Soviet model has been the MPLA (Popular Movement for the Liberation of Angola) (Somerville, 1986).

On 11 November 1975 the MPLA assumed power amid a civil war. A Marxist group who had been struggling for two decades and more to overthrow Portuguese colonial rule and establish an authentically Angolan government, they were faced with huge internal problems and hostile domestic and international opposition. The MPLA's aim to build socialism had to be carried out amid a number of struggles in the period after 1975: economic reconstruction, national unity, party-building, external armed interventions. Progress was slow in laying the foundations for a socialist society, but by the late 1970s and early 1980s the state had gained control of much of the economy, state or cooperative farms had been set up, and mass programmes of health and education had been instituted. In the political sphere, the MPLA moved to turn itself into a vanguard party along Leninist lines. However, in spite of the use of elements of the Soviet model and its adherence to Marxism–Leninism, the MPLA was never a mere puppet of Moscow, and never imported Soviet practices wholesale into Angola. The MPLA always sought to implement a local brand, fitting their own circumstances and drawn from their own political traditions and culture. Once more nationalism became fused with communism. In 1988 the USSR indicated that it could no longer afford to continue providing military assistance to the Angolans. In 1989 the MPLA and the rebel South African backed force of UNITA (led by Jonas Savimbi) agreed to a ceasefire. Subsequently, the MPLA decided to abandon Marxism–Leninism and make moves towards a multi-party system. Unfortunately, civil war broke out again not long afterwards, and the turmoil for the Angolan people continues to this day.

1989 and after . . .

The headline year for the demise of communism is often cited as 1989, when the communist dominoes all tumbled one after another in Eastern Europe in a matter of months. But as we have seen, the demise of communism and communist regimes began well before 1989. The factors vary from region to region and from country to country. If we take Eastern Europe to begin with, then it is possible to see a variety of factors at work, similar to those in the USSR. These include:

- the ongoing weaknesses in the economic sector;

- the growth of vocal dissidents and opposition movements;

- the radical change in context brought about by Gorbachev: the Sinatra doctrine and the stated willingness to allow Eastern Europe to determine its own path of development removed the fear of Soviet invasion;

- the 'demonstration effect': protests in one country led to others doing likewise as they saw the results (Fowkes, 1993: 170–77; Hudelson, 1993; Stern, 1990; Brzezinski, 1989).

Consequently, the communist regimes dissolved into thin air virtually overnight and almost without a fight. The only exceptions to this were Yugoslavia (which was gripped by brutal ethnic conflicts) and Romania. Poland went first, followed quickly by Hungary. Hungary permitted movement across its borders which pulled the rug out from under the GDR. The dismantling of the Berlin Wall led to the so-called Velvet Revolution in Prague. Romania, Bulgaria, Yugoslavia and even Albania eventually followed suit. The pattern of revolution was different in different states though. In Hungary and Poland, the transition from 'communism' to 'post-communism' was a fairly smooth transfer of power, as the communist elites voluntarily relinquished power. In East Germany and Czechoslovakia, popular uprisings put paid to the communist parties. In the Balkan states, the process was slower, more fitful and more problematic, as the communist elites proved more durable and better able to hang on to the reins of power (Fowkes, 1993: 177–94).

Elsewhere, the retreat from communism has been comprehensive, if not quite so spectacular. In China, the pro-democracy movement was brutally crushed by tanks in Tiananmen Square, and China's communists have been able to sustain their hold on power, while giving up on the goal of building communism. Similarly in Asia, Latin America and Africa, the post-war period saw the gradual displacement of communist ideals with the practical tasks of modernization, nation-building and political stability. At the start of the third millennium, there were only five states left who openly professed their allegiance to Marxism–Leninism: Cuba, North Korea, China, Vietnam and Laos. The era of communist parties and communist states dedicated to the building of communism was almost over (Sakwa, 1999). To complete this survey of communism outside the USSR, let us turn to explore the developments in the communist parties (and their ideologies) in the First World, most notably the USA and Western Europe, and examine the impact of communism upon the capitalist states.

Communism in the First World

The history of communism in the West has in many ways mirrored the history of communism elsewhere. Initially, the western left embraced the Bolshevik regime, and proclaimed the advent of a new type of civilization, superior in all respects to capitalism. With the onset of the Cold War, the revelations about Stalin and the brutal suppression of the revolts in Hungary in 1956 and Czechoslovakia in 1968, disillusionment set in among most western communists. Apart from a small rump of committed loyalists who continued to defend the USSR, western communism gradually transformed itself into a reformist movement and dropped its commitment to violent class struggle and the overthrow of capitalism.

The capitalist states felt very threatened by the emergence of Bolshevism in Russia. The news of revolution by the masses struck fear into the capitalist elites, especially during the First World War. The bold rhetoric of the Bolshevik leaders led to the western elites feeling imperilled, and during the Russian Civil War they attempted to kill the new-born regime at birth. However, while western governments were working to snuff out the Bolshevik regime, many western intellectuals, socialists, businessmen and cultural figures hailed the new regime as heralding a new type of future: a shiny, bright and just future. The USSR became a beacon for left-leaning intellectuals. A number of European socialists and communists visited the USSR in the 1920s and 1930s, either out of curiosity, or to be inspired, or to take back specific ideas that could be applied in the West. Well-known figures like George Bernard Shaw, Arthur Ransome, André Gide, Sidney and Beatrice Webb as well as leading British Labour Party politicians (for example Arthur Henderson, George Lansbury) all made the long trip to explore this 'new civilization' first-hand. Some – like John Scott, an American communist steelworker – left to go and work alongside his fellow comrades and help build the future (although Scott was very much the exception) (Scott, 1989). The lure of the Soviet Union (more so than the reality) is easily explained. The despair created by the Depression, and the fear that accompanied the rise of National Socialism left many looking for hope and salvation. The news coming out of the USSR of the rapid industrial development, the high rates of growth and the construction of huge new dams, factories, canals and metros all seemed to point to the imminent decay of capitalism and the ultimate victory of socialism and communism.

Aside from the eulogy of Sidney and Beatrice Webb (*Soviet Communism: A New Civilisation*?) published in 1935, which outlined the progressive, enlightened nature of the regime and its rulers, most fellow-travellers were not uncritical of the USSR in the 1930s but were willing to live with its blemishes, because of the depth of their belief in and commitment to the ideals of communism. This alignment was strengthened with the rise of fascism, and the fear that criticism of the USSR or Stalin, in spite of all its faults, would weaken it and aid the march of fascism. This is somewhat ironic, given that it was precisely the actions of Stalin and Comintern in preventing the German communists from collaborating with the German social democrats that was instrumental in allowing Hitler to power in the first place. The great cause célèbre of the left in the 1930s – the Spanish Civil War – seemed to confirm that a war between fascism and communism was imminent, and if fascism was to be defeated, then the USSR needed support.

Although the events of 1956 were critical in ending the love affair of western socialists and communists with the USSR, the first inklings of disillusionment came when Stalin concluded a non-aggression treaty with the Nazis in 1939. Designed to give the USSR a breathing-space, it seemed to be the clearest confirmation that the interests of the USSR would always be prior to and take precedence over the interests of the international workers movement. However, it was only after the Second World War that, with a shift in context, the balance shifted from qualified support to unqualified disillusionment and retreat. Let us briefly trace the experiences of the communist parties in the USA, Great Britain and Europe.

The communist party of the USA (like most radical left-leaning groups) has had a history of splits, mergers and general internecine strife. Its leadership and official line generally remained very closely allied to the USSR (Hudelson, 1993). There were episodes when the membership dissented from the leaders. The signing of the non-aggression treaty led many to leave the party. After the Second World War, many members felt that the leadership was not left-leaning enough, and were consequently expelled from the party. The onset of the Cold War after 1946 led to a period of sustained persecution of the CPUSA by the American state. Harry Truman instituted a loyalty oath, and the creation of The House Committee on Un-American Activities forced communists and their allies either to renounce their beliefs and provide the state with other names or face blacklisting and loss of status and earnings. The McCarthyite inquisition led to a widespread fear of communism, a fear that had been enhanced by the Soviet acquisition of the atomic bomb in 1949. The revelations of Stalin's crimes and the invasion of Hungary led to widespread disillusionment among US American communists. Membership dwindled, and although the CPUSA continues to exist, most leftist intellectuals moved to the New Left, a radical movement of social protest against Vietnam, pro-civil rights and pro free speech on US campuses. Despite participating in US presidential elections since 1968, the CPUSA has failed to make any electoral headway, either locally or nationally.

A very similar story can be seen in the UK, whereby, apart from a brief period at the end of the Second World War, the CPGB (along with other splinter left-wing groups) has failed to make a significant electoral impact (Sassoon, 1997; Callaghan,

1987; Woodhouse & Pearce, 1975). The CPGB was formed out of a series of mergers and splits in the 1920s and 1930s, and had their first MP elected in 1935. Initially, the CPGB opposed the war, but when Nazi Germany invaded the USSR the CPGB campaigned actively for a Second Front and justified its stance by the need to defeat fascism. The 1945 General Election brought the CPGB two parliamentary seats and a total of 103,000 votes. This was the high watermark of British communism. The 1950s were a decade of transition. The CPGB drew up a ground-breaking document, *The British Road to Socialism*, in 1951. This advocated a peaceful, parliamentary transition to socialism, while remaining instinctively pro-Soviet (Callaghan, 1987: 164). The year 1956 was one that dealt a huge, fatal blow to the CPGB. The combined impact of Khrushchev's 'secret speech' and the crushing of the Hungarian Revolution led to mass resignations from the party. The British New Left was born at this point, a movement of 'revisionist' intellectuals who sought to combine different strands of humanistic and ethical socialism and Marxism. The main theoretical journal of the British New Left was *New Left Review*, which explored a range of new thinkers and approaches, including questions of culture, and the ideas of Antonio Gramsci and the Frankfurt School. Increasingly, the CPGB came to be little more than a group exerting pressure on the Labour Party. The revolutionary mantle passed to groups such as the Revolutionary Communist Party (RCP) and the Socialist Workers' Party (SWP). The party became riven with factions, and in 1991 the reformist leadership decided to disband it, and renamed itself the Democratic Left. A group of orthodox communists reconstituted the party and reaffirmed their belief in the communist ideal. In their party programme of 2005, they continue to define their ultimate goal as the construction of a communist society, along the lines of that set out by Marx and Engels.

While the fate of communism in the USA and the UK has been one of in-fighting, and progressive marginalization and irrelevance, the history of communism in Western Europe is very different. The two most successful were the Italian Communist Party (PCI) and the French Communist Party (PCF), both of which were to play significant roles in the post-war politics of their countries (Sassoon, 1997; Lichtheim, 1975; Ulassi, 1969). The general contours of their histories are very similar to those of the Anglo-American communists, with 1956 also being a watershed of disillusionment with the USSR. Up until that point, they had remained, on the whole, staunch, loyal, internationalist allies of the USSR. After 1956, the Western European communist parties started divorce proceedings from Moscow. The split was acrimonious. Gradually, each party did not just move away from the CPSU, but also away from each other. Autonomy from Moscow became national communism, as each party became increasingly concerned with its own local political context, cultures, traditions and demands. This 'drift' led to the parties doing two things: questioning many of the fundamental tenets of goal and organization they had inherited from the CPSU, and replacing it with a new set of ideals and structures. The upshot of this was the emergence of Eurocommunism in the 1970s, which was given extra impetus by the crushing of the Prague Spring in 1968 (Della Torre, Mortimer & Story, 1979).

The phase of questioning led the European communists to abandon the belief in violent revolution and class struggle led by a vanguard party as the way to make the transition from capitalism to socialism and communism. In its stead, the

Eurocommunists posited a belief in the power of structural reforms to capitalism to bring about socialism, and of mass political parties participating in democratic institutions and operating according to the rules of parliamentary democracy. In a joint declaration of the French and Italian Communist parties issued on 15 November 1975, it was noted that

[t]he Italian and French communists hold that the march towards socialism and the building of a socialist society, which they propose as the prospect for their countries, must be achieved within the framework of continuous democratisation of economic, social and political life.
(Della Torre, Mortimer & Story, 1979: 335)

But Eurocommunism failed to halt the electoral slide of the European communist parties, as they struggled to maintain their position in the political mainstream. The Italian communists dissolved themselves in 1991, and turned into the *Partito Democratico della Sinistra* (Democratic Party of the Left) and the *Partito della Rifondazione Comunista* (Communist Reformation Party). The demise of the PCF seemed to be confirmed by its performance in the first round of the French presidential elections in April 2002, when Robert Hue trailed in 11th with only 3.4% of the vote, some way behind Jacques Chirac (19.9%) and the Far Right figure of Jean-Marie Le Pen (16.9%). Apart from a brief period in the 1960s and 1970s on mainland Europe, communism has made little political headway, whether measured in terms of membership of the party or electoral success (either nationally or locally). But is it possible to examine the impact – positive and negative – that communist ideas, communist figures, communist parties and communist regimes may have had on life in the West? In what ways did communism make itself felt in the West?

The potential parameters of this appraisal are enormous, so I will restrict this part to some general comments. One of the ironies of this era in human history is that an ideology expressly committed to the destruction and overthrow of capitalism may have contributed, unwittingly, to its longevity. Communism (and leftist movements in general) compelled capitalism to adopt a more reformist approach, taking greater account of the welfare and living standards of the people. This approach has contributed to capitalism's own ability to adapt and reform itself, thus making it more stable in the long run. Additionally, communist parties and states also contributed to the survival of capitalism and liberal democracy when faced with its greatest challenges: the Depression and fascism. By splitting the left in the 1930s, the USSR contributed to the rise of the right, but also seriously weakened the socialists and communists at a time when capitalism appeared to be tottering. Moreover, the Soviet resistance and eventual defeat of the Nazis were crucial in the long-term victory over fascism during the Second World War.

Did communism also inadvertently contribute to the survival of capitalism in the Cold War? It has been argued that the existence of an external 'enemy', an identifiable 'other', is often used by states as a means of political legitimation and to offset criticisms and explain away internal problems (in exactly the way that the communist regimes sought to blame all their ills on the 'forces of imperialism' or 'vestiges of capitalism'). Communism provided the 'other' which was used as a 'glue' to bind the people to the elites in the capitalist societies. But capitalism was also profoundly transformed socially and culturally by the rivalry with communism during the Cold War, becoming increasingly militarized and security-conscious. But which was cause and which effect? Did the existence of a global communist system ostensibly committed to world revolution force a militarization of capitalist society? Or did the existence of communism provide the rationale for greater controls and a more militaristic ethos, allowing the military–industrial complex the opportunity to increase its leverage over resource allocations?

Interestingly, in the eyes of capitalist societies, it was also the failings of communism which helped the capitalist democracies. The consistently poor showing of the communist economies after 1945 seemed to demonstrate the superiority of capitalism. It has been said that the performance of the capitalist economies since the 1960s only looks good when set alongside the performance of the Soviet command economies. Judged on its own merits, rather than in comparison, it would undoubtedly have received a much harsher judgement.

The Cold War was an unmitigated disaster for humanity and for the planet, and the communist regimes and parties in power must carry their (large) share of responsibility. This global competition between the two systems led to enormous waste and horrific mortality rates, primarily in the developing world. There is not enough space here to talk about where responsibility lies for the onset and development of the Cold War. Each side has its own passionate advocates. Each side played a part, even if it was only in an overreaction to an action of the other side, or in language which demonized the other, legitimating the atmosphere of hostility and dogmatism. It will take a while for the emergence of scholars and scholarship one step removed from the struggles of the Cold War to start a more dispassionate appraisal. The Cold War did inadvertently produce some positive spin-offs: the global competition did spur on some human achievements: sporting, technological, the space race and so on, but the overall balance-sheet is overwhelmingly negative.

While many communists in the capitalist countries were obedient agents of Moscow, and looked only to destroy the capitalist way of life, increasingly since 1956 and the disillusionment with Soviet power many communists have turned instead to the role of critic and herald, advocates for peace, disarmament and social justice. These critics, along with many others of course, have been central in attempts to combat those elements of global capitalism – injustice, inequality, unemployment, environmental degradation, oppression and exploitation – which continue to blight the lives of many ordinary people. The existence of plural voices, of dissenting views, is a crucial and enriching part of the appeal of democratic civil society, and provides liberalism with one of its greatest challenges: how, if at all, should you tolerate those who would wish to criticize and overturn your way of life?

In cultural terms, many key cultural figures in the West either have been inspired by, or their work has been informed by, their communist beliefs, activities or sympathies, and western culture has also been profoundly influenced by the cultural output of many writers, artists, poets and film-makers who lived under communism (without necessarily being communist). In the West, the early writings of Jean-Paul Sartre and Albert Camus were inspired by their faith in communism. Similarly, the poetry of Pablo Neruda was underpinned by his communist ideals. The life and works of Pablo Picasso are an interesting example of the cultural production of someone deeply committed to the communist cause. Picasso joined the PCF in 1944, but refused to adopt slavishly the policy of Socialist Realism. Picasso worked tirelessly to promote communism and the international peace movement, either through donating money or works of art, or through constructing numerous party posters. Picasso also produced overtly political paintings, such as the 'Massacre in Korea' (1951). Perhaps the most well-known image associated with Picasso was the dove which he reworked on numerous occasions as the symbol of the international peace movement (Utley, 2000).

The culture of early Soviet communism produced some innovative and intriguing work which is notable in the history of twentieth-century culture. The work of people such as the poets Mayakovsky and Blok, the artists Isaak Brodski, Alexander Rodchenko and Kazimir Malevich, writers such as Maksim Gorky and Mikhail Sholokhov, cinema directors like Sergei Eisenstein and Lev Kuleshov, and the music of composer Dmitri Shostakovich have all been influential in different ways (Gleason, 1985; Kelly & Shepherd, 1998; Read, 1990). The 1920s also produced a variety of weird and wonderful utopian speculation and experimentation in fields like architecture, town-planning, science-fiction, fashion, and children's names (Stites, 1989; Fitzpatrick, 1978). Unfortunately, the imposition of a rigid and dogmatic blanket over the cultural sphere virtually suffocated the creativity in Soviet culture, at least on the surface. From the 1930s onwards, in the USSR and later on in Eastern Europe, communism produced notable cultural figures. However, rather than being inspired by the energy and hope of the revolution, these cultural producers were reacting against the vagaries of communist oppression and propaganda. Figures like Boris Pasternak, Osip Mandelstam, Czeslaw Milosz, Vaclav Havel, Aleksander Solzhenitsyn, Joseph Brodsky, Anna Akhmatova, Jaroslav Hasek, Vladimir Voinovich, Irina Ratushinskaya all developed sustained critical and/or satirical portraits of the communist regime, primarily, but not exclusively, from a humanist perspective. The degrading and dehumanizing experience of living under the brutal communist regimes created a great deal of work – literary, musical, artistic – which celebrates the human spirit and its unwillingness to tolerate oppression and injustice.

Conclusion: Communism across the globe 1945–2005

Summing up the experience of communism outside the USSR after 1945, one can point to a general trend whereby communist influence and control expanded rapidly after 1945, but began to decline from the mid-1950s, leading to its rapid collapse and dissolution as a movement and as states in the late 1980s and early 1990s. But the decline and fall of international communism came about for a variety of reasons. First, communism for most states outside the USSR was a developmental path that was chosen because it fitted with the particular circumstances of that country: either as part of the modernization process or part of the national-liberation struggle, or as a means of acquiring resources for nation-building. It was usually linked to a particular goal or aim and, once this aim had been met, the *raison d'être* for the adoption of the Soviet model disappeared. Secondly, there was an inherent tension in the emergence of a polycentric communist bloc: nationalism and communism sat uneasily side by side. Gradually, nationalism began to displace communism. Thirdly, belief in communism began to wane because of a growing sense of disillusionment with the USSR. It no longer seemed able or willing to deliver a shiny, bright future of prosperity and freedom. Instead it began to look more and more like a system in retreat and growing stagnant. Finally, communism was also caught up in postmodernism's revolt against grand narratives: the whole story no longer seemed credible or relevant in the West and had failed to deliver in the East. The communist era was over.

Recommended reading

Good overviews of the decline of international communism include: G. Stern, *The Rise and Decline of International Communism* (Edward Elgar, 1990); R. Sakwa, *Postcommunism* (Open University Press, 1999); R. Hudelson, *The Rise and Fall of Communism* (Westview Press, 1993); Z. Brzezinski, *The Grand Failure* (Macdonald, 1990).

On Eastern Europe, see: B. Fowkes, *The Rise and Fall of Communism in Eastern Europe* (Macmillan, 1993); R.J. Crampton, *Eastern Europe in the Twentieth Century and After* (Routledge, 1994). On China, see A. Dirlik, *The Origins of Chinese Communism* (OUP, 1989); B. Brugger (ed.), *The Impact of the Cultural Revolution* (Croom Helm, 1978). A controversial new work is J. Halliday and Jung Chang, *Mao: The Untold Story* (Random House, 2005). A good comparative piece is D. Treadgold (ed.), *Soviet and Chinese Communism: Similarities and Differences* (University of Washington Press, 1967). Asian communism is best looked at by country: M. Beresford, *Vietnam: Politics, Economics, Society* (Pinter, 1988); K.D. Jackson (ed.), *Cambodia 1975–78* (Princeton University Press, 1989). For Cuba, see I. Horowitz (ed.), *Cuban Communism* (Transaction Publishers, 1989). For Chile, see R.J. Alexander, *The Tragedy of Chile* (Greenwood Press, 1978). For Angola, see K. Somerville, *Angola: Politics, Economics, Society* (Pinter, 1986). D. Sassoon, *One Hundred Years of Socialism* (Fontana, 1997); P. della Torre, E. Mortimer and J. Story (eds), *Eurocommunism: Myth or Reality?* (Penguin, 1979); H. Klehr, *The Secret World of American Communism* (Yale University Press, 1995); G. Utley, *Pablo Picasso: The Communist Years* (Yale University Press, 2000).

CHAPTER 6

Conclusion

The communist leopard frequently changes its spots, but the same blood – bad blood – continuously flows through its veins.

J. Edgar Hoover

Introduction

REFLECTING ON THE HISTORY OF communism, a number of questions spring to mind. Why did it collapse? What legacy has it left? How should history judge it? And what, if anything, is the future for communism? Answering these questions takes us into some dangerous, deeply contested and fairly hostile waters. There has been an at times rather unwholesome fight over the communist corpse. Some wish to bury it out of sight; others wish to decapitate it and parade its head on a big stick, mocking, condemning and deriding it; alternatively, some have tried to give it a more dignified send-off, without really mourning it. Few, if any, have either wished to give it a valedictory eulogy, or wistfully regretted its passing. To conclude this brief review of the history of communism, let us try to answer some of these questions. Let us reflect first of all on a key question: why did almost all the communist regimes fall apart in the late twentieth century?

Reflection One: Why did communism fall/collapse/be overthrown?

This is a complex question, in common with all similar sorts of attempts to explain the decline or fall or collapse or overthrow of other civilizations: the Roman Empire, the Ottoman Empire or Tsarist Russia. The answers that have been provided have tended to identify a series of factors which were crucial in undermining the communist regimes:

- economic slowdown/failure;

- widespread corruption;

- growing pessimism/alienation/cynicism among the people;

- disillusionment with the communist elites;

- total loss of faith in the ideology: gap between promises and reality;

- dissidence and growing unrest (political, social, national);

- military defeat in Afghanistan;

- resurgence of Islam in Iran and elsewhere;

- growing gap with the West: technologically, militarily, in levels of consumption.

All these factors (and more) are rightly cited in explanations of the fall of communism. But these 'lists' of factors are insufficient. They are at once both too general and too specific. Too general because they fail to explain why communism fell *at that time* and *in that way*, and also do not show how these factors relate to each other. Too specific because they don't really get to the question of why all these factors had appeared in the first place.

So let us try to answer these two further questions. The issue of *why then* and *in that way* cannot be answered except with reference to the actions of individuals, accidents, and the conjunction of particular circumstances. Crucial in this regard clearly are the Chernobyl accident, the advent of Gorbachev and the sequence and evolution of his reform agenda, the mistakes and miscalculations he made, the spat with Yeltsin, as well as the actions of the border guards in East Germany in hastening the demise of the Berlin Wall. The factors listed previously were necessary for its collapse, but by themselves they were not enough. Most scholars contend that, although the communist economic and political systems were struggling, they were still fundamentally viable, at least in the short–medium term. What precipitated the fall at that time were the actions and accidents after 1986. Scholars do differ though over whether the events after 1986 were causal, or catalytic. One school of thought contends that the system was ill, but not dying. However, the medicine administered by Gorbachev, and its unforeseen side-effects, killed the communist patient. A different school of thought contends that the patient was terminally ill, and Gorbachev et al. merely hastened its demise through administering flawed medicine resulting from a wrong-headed diagnosis.

But even those who agree that the system was in terminal decline disagree over why it was so sick, a sickness which was manifesting itself in the symptoms outlined above. Why did these factors appear in the first place? In other words, what were the underlying – political, philosophical, ideological, socio-economic – reasons for its sickness? For Richard Pipes, the answer is clear-cut:

We are now in a position to address the question . . . whether the failure of communism 'was due to human error or to flaws inherent in its very nature.' The record of history strongly suggests the latter to be the case. Communism was not a good idea that went wrong; it was a bad idea.
(Pipes, 2002: 147)

The roots of this, according to Pipes, lay in a 'genetic flaw' in Marxism which rested on two erroneous propositions: that private property was destined to die out, and that human beings can be fashioned and refashioned at will. When communist regimes found it impossible to do this, it ended by creating huge coercive, rigid, bureaucratic leviathans to try to enforce this new type of civilization. For Pipes, the resulting systems were thus fundamentally flawed, both domestically and internationally. Domestically, the communist systems – set up to create freedom and equality – actually created a society of tyranny and inequality which destroyed its legitimacy and credibility. But this system was also unreformable: it was locked together as a self-contained, self-supporting whole. It was not possible to tinker with or change one or more parts of it. The whole system proved impervious to change, unable to adapt and so it collapsed as soon as the use or threat of coercion was lifted by Gorbachev. Internationally, communism failed because ethnic and territorial loyalties proved more durable and attractive than class ones. Nationalism vanquished international communism and even displaced Marxism–Leninism in most communist parties in power (Pipes, 2002).

A different approach is taken by others such as Richard Sakwa, Walter Laqueur and Shmuel Eisenstadt. Laqueur rejects the approach of Pipes, arguing that the leap from Marx and Marxism to the specifics of the communist regime after 1917 is too big and too unhistorical to make convincingly. Instead, Laqueur posits that the system was doomed in the long run by its inability to make good on its promises, but that its downfall (like its emergence in the first place) was due to a series of historical accidents (Laqueur, 1994). Sakwa and Eisenstadt in comparison also deny that the intellectual origins of communism were the ultimate reasons for its downfall. Instead, they point to the 'mismodernization' or 'flawed' modernization undertaken after 1917. Sakwa argues that the communist regimes developed some of the main aspects of modernity (industrialization, urbanization, literate population), but the pattern of development stunted the full onset of modernity:

[the] fundamental features of effective modernisation were missing: the bias against innovation, the emphasis on quantitative growth; low productivity of labour; enormous waste and poor quality; lack of co-ordination . . . (Sakwa, 1999: 25)

The pattern of development chosen by the Bolsheviks and other communists – a product of the specific ideological, historical and cultural context of the time of their emergence – lay at the root of this 'mismodernization'. Likewise, in the political sphere, the communist regimes were unable to develop viable systems which were inclusive, stable and able to manage ethnic and national tensions. Summing up, Sakwa argues that

[a]bove all, communism failed to resolve the core problem that it set itself, namely the overcoming of alienation and the achievement of freedom. Communism was indeed in agonia, *mental anguish at the gulf between its ideals, the reality it found itself in and the reality it became.*
(Sakwa, 1999: 25)

Common to most interpretations of the roots of the failure of communism is this 'gap' between their oft-professed ideals and the reality that they constructed and presided over. By the late 1970s, hardly anyone outside the elites believed in the system, had faith in it, wished to defend it, or thought it could deliver on its promises (and many within the elite had lost their faith too). It unravelled really quickly because, well, no one wanted it to carry on any more. But what caused this flawed reality to emerge in the first place? While it is clear that the mental structures, patterns of thinking and policy preferences implicit within the Marxist–Leninist framework were key in shaping the system and its responses, it is too reductionist to seek the origins of the accumulating problems solely or primarily in a nineteenth-century, Enlightenment-inspired, hyper-rational world-view. The reasons for the poor performance of the system, and the creation of a system which was almost the antithesis of that which it set out to reach have to be rooted in cultural and historical specifics as well as personalities and accidents: civil war, world war, cultures, traditions and mentalities, premature deaths of key individuals. The overall evolution of each communist system needs to be considered, as does the changing international context: war, intervention, economic crisis, Cold War, military defeat. All these things have to be factored in if we are to explain – fully, convincingly and holistically – the reasons behind the fall from power of each communist regime. To outline a straight, unbroken line from the Enlightenment, through Marx, Engels and Lenin to Stalin, is really too neat, too formulaic. There was not one preordained outcome of 1917. History is far messier and more complex than that.

A related question concerns the extent/sincerity of belief in the system and its ideology from within the elite itself: why did this erode so fast? Pipes contends that in fact once communist regimes have been established, self-interest, personal aggrandisement, naked ambition and political survival become the dominant imperatives, not the ideas that inspired the revolution in the first place (Pipes, 2002). Clearly the intensity of belief diminished noticeably across the decades, and there were very few 'true' believers left by the end, which does tend to reinforce the notion that there were very few people left willing to defend the system, except those who continued to benefit materially from its continuation.

Reflection Two: How will history judge communism?

Another debate that has generated great heat (but not quite so much light) is the one over the historical record of communism, and in particular the question of how we might judge it. This takes us into the territory occupied by the *Black Book of Communism* among others, as well as the rather murky and sometimes distasteful debates about just how many people were killed by communism (and capitalism), and the relative awfulness of communism v. fascism. It also raises broader questions about the place of judgement in history and the issue of whether or not an ism can be held responsible for the killing of millions of people.

The key texts in this regard have been those of Courtois et al. (mentioned above) and also that of François Furet, *The Passing of An Illusion: The Idea of Communism in the Twentieth Century*. What marked out both these texts was that they sought to put communism on trial, to judge its historical record. In each case the author/s were prosecution counsel, not defence. In each case there was little, if any, case for the defence. There were no mitigating circumstances submitted, no countervailing evidence, no witnesses for the defence. The books, and especially the Courtois volume, restrict themselves to a detailed listing of the crimes of communism and finish with a piece of historical accounting, adding up the number of victims to reach the 'magic' figure of 100 million deaths because of communism. A figure guaranteed to make headlines.

Furet's work was written from an anti-communist standpoint. His premise was that communism rested on an illusion: 'the idea of salvation through history' (Furet, 2004: ix). This belief that a perfect society of freedom and justice and equality was just around the corner was the powerful moving force which persuaded many to make a massive personal and psychological investment in this ideal. He details the brutal, destructive elements of communism in the twentieth century, and argues that the power of communism to attract supporters lay in its message of anti-fascism, and in the reality of the Soviet defeat of National Socialism between 1941 and 1945. The Courtois volume went one stage further than that of Furet. Its entire focus was on the central, essential aspect of communism: its criminal nature.

The *Black Book* contains a (controversial) introduction and conclusion from Courtois himself, as well as chapters on the USSR (Nicolas Werth); world revolution and terror (Courtois, Jean-Louis

Panne and Remi Kauffer); Eastern Europe (Andrjez Packowski and Karel Bartosek); Asia (Jean-Louis Margolinand Pierre Rigolout) and the Third World (Pascal Fontaine, Yves Santamaria and Sylvain Boulouque). The entire project is designed to criminalize communism and so undercut forever any political project which might share its ideals. Courtois's final body count of almost 100 million was deeply contested, not least by some of the other authors in the book, as he notably revised upwards the figures given for the USSR, Vietnam and Latin America! Underpinning Courtois's analysis is his desire to draw parallels with Nazism and to note (like Pipes) the exceptional, criminal nature of communism and its genetic linkage with the 'messianic dimension of the Marxist project to reunify humanity via the proletariat' (Courtois, 1999: 747).

Both Courtois and Pipes sought to highlight the essential similarities between communism and fascism. Courtois noted that:

[t]he future Nazi society was to be built upon a 'pure race', and the future communist society was to be built upon a proletarian people purified of the dregs of the bourgeoisie. The restructuring of these two societies was envisioned in the same way, even if the crackdowns were different. Therefore, it would be foolish to pretend that Communism is a form of universalism. Communism may have a worldwide purpose, but like Nazism it deems a part of humanity unworthy of existence. The difference is that the communist model is based on the class system, the Nazi model on race and territory. (Courtois, 1999: 16)

Similarly, Pipes maintains that the affinities between Nazism and Stalinism (both species of totalitarian regimes) run very deep. They had a common enemy (liberal democracy) and Stalin provided a model of one-party rule which Hitler was able to use and apply in Germany.

But the political project of Courtois to conflate Nazism and communism has been deeply criticized, most notably because it is a project driven entirely by ideology rather than historical analysis and comparison. As Aronson has so clearly detailed, both Margolin and Werth rejected Courtois's attempts to draw comparisons with Nazism (Aronson, 2003). Margolin argued that there was a basic and fundamental difference in the orientation and essence of the two systems: communism called for human liberation, Nazism for racial extermination. David Joravsky outlined the concrete differences between fascism/Nazism and communism, specifically focusing upon the conditions of their emergence, their goals, longevity and their attitudes to war and economic development (Joravsky, 1994). Sakwa has also noted that, while there is clearly a crude similarity in terms of body counts, the approach and essence of the regimes were quite distinct. The goals of the communist regimes were on the whole benign (even if the reality quite clearly was not) (Sakwa, 1999). Similarly, the approach which takes totalitarianism as the starting point has been criticized for lacking historical specificity when analyzing the reality of the differing forms of communism. Joravsky has argued that totalitarianism was little more than a crusade undertaken to discredit all movements opposed to the western model of liberal-democratic capitalism, and so is of little if any use in understanding or analyzing real, complex historical phenomena.

In essence, the key criticism of those who have sought to prosecute and judge communism has been precisely this intention. A prosecution case is not good history if it takes no account of context, motivation and countervailing evidence. Providing the details of the crimes of communism, horrific and brutal though they clearly were, should not replace historical analysis and under-standing. Although Courtois mentions the culture of violence, war and militarism out of which Bolshevism and National Socialism grew, this is not cited as being of import when explaining the actions of the communists. It is this absence of both an international context (war, civil war, world war, Cold War) and a domestic context (native traditions and cul-tures in Russia and China) which renders much of the *Black Book* so one-sided and therefore an ideologically driven distortion. However, it is not just the absence of context which is the problem. It also lacks specificity. Communism is lumped together as one homogenous mass. Is it really accurate to put together the PCF and the Khmer Rouge? Allende and Mao? The Sandinistas and Kim Il Jong? The plural nature of communism, along with its evolution both internationally and domestically, needs to be considered.

A rounded analysis must take account of all aspects of com-munism: its achievements and successes, as well as its failures and the terrible price paid by millions of people across the globe. Any analysis of communism must try to understand (as well as document and condemn) why the regimes under Stalin, Mao and Pol Pot killed millions of people. But that analysis must also include the measures to modernize, educate, implement health care, abolish poverty and so on. The question should also be asked about how far the millions killed can be attributed to 'communism'. Can an ideology kill? Would it not be more appro-priate to argue that it is people who kill? Are not the 'crimes of communism' really, ultimately, the crimes of Stalin? Of Mao? Of Pol Pot? Of individual officials, policemen, troops etc. who staffed the regimes and engaged in countless acts of micro-brutality?

Are we also not guilty of double standards? Aronson argues that the same standards should be applied to capitalism. The *Black Book of Capitalism* details over 100 million deaths from wars, mass murders, colonial violence, and famines which can be laid at the feet of capitalism. Does this alter our historical perception of communism, even if it does not take away the revulsion at the horrors of communism? Clearly, a case can be made that it is unfair and inappropriate to blame capitalism for many of these deaths. Can we blame capitalism for the Armenian genocide? The ethnic cleansing in Rwanda? But the same criteria need to be applied to communism as well. Indeed, the whole context of the Cold War conflict between capitalism and communism needs to be foregrounded in any analysis of the historical record of communism.

Any brief survey of the lives of the ordinary citizens of the former communist countries will demonstrate the mixed blessings that the end of communism has brought. Overall, a start needs to be made on developing an historically grounded, contextually specific analysis of communism in all of its historical, cultural and geographical variations, one which has left behind the stereotypes of Cold War thinking, but which embraces the critical impact that the Cold War had in conditioning the nature of the two systems. It is an analysis that must document the deaths and brutality of communism, and all other aspects of the communist system too.

Reflection Three: The future of communism?

What future for communism? This short text has explored the *longue durée* of communism, as an ideal and as an alternative, as a critique and a protest against existing patterns of inequality, domination and exploitation, and finally as a political movement and as a regime in power which came to dominate large parts of the globe in the twentieth century but which has virtually disappeared in the twenty-first century. So, does communism have a future?

The model and pattern of the communist regimes which emerged, grew and fell between 1917 and 1991 will hopefully not be seen again. The whole model is discredited, bankrupt and anachronistic. In some senses this is not unexpected. When 'modern' communism emerged in the nineteenth century, it was both a critique of modernity and an attempt to transcend modernity. As the 'modern' era begins to fade away, it seems fitting that the communist movement and the model of communist regime should also disappear. However, what about the idea of communism, the yearning for a better, fairer world of equality, justice and freedom? Has this idea died with it? Has the postmodern ennui with big ideas – liberalism, socialism, Marxism, communism – destroyed the possibility of a revival of communist ideas and values? The problems besetting communism are of a two-fold nature. First, there are problems of a temporal nature. The experience of communism in power is still too recent for it to be considered a viable alternative to the current arrangements. Second, there are problems at a philosophical level. Communism is illusory because it will never, according to Pipes, be able to overcome the inherent selfishness and acquisitiveness of human nature. All projects, on this reading, which hope to remake society on a communal, cooperative, altruistic basis are doomed to fail (Pipes, 2002: 160–61). So must we bury the idea as well?

Not yet. If we go back to the roots of communism, it first emerged (in its pre-modern form) as a *critique* of the inequalities and exploitation of the existing society, and as an *alternative* – either in the realms of fantastical theorizing or small-scale experimentation – to that society. Well, the current global situation, and the nature of late capitalism do suggest that the need for a collectivist critique of capitalism and its practices is as great as ever. While certain sections of the global population continue to enjoy ever increasing standards of living, this experience is not shared by the vast majority of the population across the world. The manifold failure of capitalism to overcome poverty and inequality, and indeed the growing levels of inequality between rich and poor (both within the developed economies and between the developed and the less developed nations) both testify to this (Sakwa, 1999). The whole thrust of late capitalism with its hyper-individualism and consumerism is deeply corrosive of the social ties, obligations and ethics of duty that keep societies together. Communism, or at least a critique of capitalism which stresses the collective and the cooperative, is as necessary now as it has ever been.

Secondly, the human spirit is constantly thinking, dreaming and speculating about alternative, better futures. As Furet has argued,

we are, condemned to live in the world as it is. This condition is too austere and contrary to the spirit of modern societies to last. Democracy, by virtue of its existence, creates the need for a world . . . in which a genuine human community can flourish . . . But the end of the Soviet world in no way alters the democratic call for another society . . .
(Furet, 2004: 502)

The aspiration to create something better, to build something new will continue to bring forth not just critiques of the dominant modes of thinking and the dominant ways of organizing society: this is likely, given the current hegemony of individualistic capitalism, to be speculations and dreams of a communal nature, albeit very different from that we have seen up until now.

Finally, the question of the philosophical impossibility or otherwise, based upon perceptions of human nature. It is equally possible to make a case that human beings are inherently sociable and always find collaborative forms to express themselves, to solve problems and cooperate in achieving collective goals. Humans are communal and personal, sociable and individualistic, selfish and selfless. Each society throughout human history has thrown up examples of collective experiments and acts of great selflessness and altruism. The great curiosity is not whether communism will return at some point, but what it will look like and what historical circumstances are likely to give rise to it. To these questions there are yet no answers. Let the dreaming begin.

Recommended reading

A variety of pieces have sought to write communism's obituary or review its history. See, for example: R. Pipes, *Communism* (Phoenix, 2002); W. Laqueur, *The Dream That Failed* (OUP, 1994); R. Sakwa, *Postcommunism* (Open University Press, 1999); G. Stern, *The Rise and Decline of International Communism* (Edward Elgar, 1990); Z. Brzezinski, *The Grand Failure* (Macdonald, 1990); R. Hudelson, *The Rise and Fall of Communism* (Westview Press, 1993); F. Furet, *The Passing of An Illusion*, (University of Chicago Press, 1999); S. Courtois et al., *The Black Book of Communism* (Harvard University Press, 1999); S. Eisenstadt, 'The

breakdown of communist regimes and the vicissitudes of modernity',
in *Daedalus*, 121 vol. 2, Spring 1992, pp. 21–41; L. Kolakowski, 'Amidst
moving ruins', in ibid., pp. 43–56; D. Joravsky, 'Communism in historical
perspective', in *American Historical Review*, June 1994, pp. 837–57;
R. Aronson, 'Communism's posthumous trial', in *History and Theory*,
42 (May 2003), pp. 222–45.

Abbreviations

CC	Central Committee
CCP	Chinese Communist Party
CHEKA	Extraordinary Commission for the Suppression of Counter-Revolutionary Speculation and Sabotage
COMECON	Council for Mutual Economic Assistance
COMINFORM	Communist Information Bureau
COMINTERN	Communist International
CPGB	Communist Party of Great Britain
CPSU	Communist Party of the Soviet Union
GDR	German Democratic Republic
GLF	Great Leap Forward
GOSPLAN	State Planning Commission
IWMA	International Working Men's Association
KGB	Committee of State Security
KWP	Korean Workers' Party
MPLA	Popular Movement for the Liberation of Angola
NATO	North Atlantic Treaty Organization
NEP	New Economic Policy
NKVD	People's Commissariat for Internal Affairs
PCF	Communist Party of France

PCI	Communist Party of Italy
RCP	Russian Communist Party
RSDLP	Russian Social Democratic Labour Party
SPD	Social Democratic Party (Germany)
USSR	Union of Soviet Socialist Republics
VESENKHA	Supreme Council of the National Economy

References

Alexander, R.J. (1978), *The Tragedy of Chile*, Westport, CT: Greenwood Press.

Aronson, Raymond (2003), 'Communism's posthumous trial', *History and Theory*, 42, May 2003, 222–45.

Bacon, Edwin and Sandle, Mark (eds) (2002), *Brezhnev Reconsidered*, Basingstoke: Palgrave.

Beller, D.C. and Rejai, M. (1969), 'Communism in Sub-Saharan Africa', in Dan Jacobs (ed.), *The New Communisms*, New York: Harper and Row.

Beresford, M. (1988), *Vietnam: Politics, Economics, Society*, London: Pinter.

Blecher, M. (1986), *China*, London: Pinter.

Brown, Archie (1996), *The Gorbachev Factor*, Oxford: Oxford University Press.

Brugger, B. (ed.) (1978), *China: The Impact of the Cultural Revolution*, London: Croom Helm.

Brzezinski, Zbigniew (1989), *The Grand Failure*, London: Macdonald.

Bukharin, Nikolai and Preobrazhensky, Evgenii (1969), *ABC of Communism*, Harmondsworth: Penguin.

Callaghan, J. (1987), *The Far Left in British Politics*, Oxford: Basil Blackwell.

Campanella, Tomasso (1981), *La Città del Sole*, California: University of California Press.

Carey, J. (ed.) (1999), *The Faber Book of Utopias*, London: Faber and Faber.

Carr, E.H. (1966), *The Bolshevik Revolution 1917–23* [vol. 2], Harmondsworth: Penguin.

Cole, G.D.H. (1958), *A History of Socialist Thought* [vol. 1], Basingstoke: Macmillan.

Courtois, Stephane et al. (1999), *The Black Book of Communism*, Cambridge, MA: Harvard University Press.

CPSU (1961), *The Road to Communism*, Moscow: Foreign Languages Publishing House.

Crampton, Richard, J. (1994), *Eastern Europe in the Twentieth Century and After*, London: Routledge.

Cranston, Maurice (1991), *Jean-Jacques: The Early Life and Work of Jean-Jacques Roussean 1712–1754*, Chicago: University of Chicago Press.

Cranston, Maurice (1999), *The Solitary Self: Jean-Jacques Roussean in Exile and Adversity*, Chicago: University of Chicago Press.

Degras, J. (ed.) (1971), *The Communist International 1919–43* [in 3 volumes: 1919–22; 1922–28; and 1929–43], London: Cass.

Della Torre, P., Mortimer, E. and **Story, J.** (eds) (1979), *Eurocommunism: Myth or Reality?*, Harmondsworth: Penguin.

Dirlik, A. (1989), *The Origins of Chinese Communism*, Oxford: OUP.

Engels, Friedrich (1847a), 'Draft of a communist confession of faith', in Marx and Engels Collected Works [MECW] [vol. 6], London: Lawrence and Wishart, 1976.

Engels, Friedrich (1847b), 'Principles of communism', in MECW [vol. 6], London: Lawrence and Wishart, 1976.

Feifer, George (1975), 'No protest: The case of the passive minority', in Tokes, Rudolf. L. (ed.), *Dissent in the USSR*, Baltimore: Johns Hopkins University Press.

Filtzer, Donald (1993), *The Khrushchev Era: De-Stalinisation and the Limits of Reform in the USSR 1953–64*, Basingstoke: Macmillan.

Fitzpatrick, Sheila (ed.) (1978), *Cultural Revolution in Russia 1928–31*, Bloomington: Indiana University Press.

Fowkes, Ben (1993), *The Rise and Fall of Communism in Eastern Europe*, Basingstoke: Macmillan.

Frank, P. (1979), *The Fourth International*, London: Ink Links.

Furet, François (2004), *The Passing of An Illusion*, Chicago: University of Chicago Press.

George, de R. (1981), 'Marxism and the good society', in Burke, J.P., Crocker, L. and Legters, L. (eds), *Marxism and the Good Society*, Cambridge: Cambridge University Press.

Gil, Federico (1969), 'Communism in Latin America', in Jacobs, Dan (ed.), *The New Communisms*, New York: Harper and Row.

Gleason, Abbot, et al. (eds) (1985), *Bolshevik Culture: Experiment and Order in the Russian Revolution*, Bloomington: Indiana University Press.

Gorbachev, Mikhail (1986), *Report to the 27th CPSU Congress*, Moscow: Novosti Press.

Gorbachev, Mikhail (1989), 'Sotsialisticheskaya ideya i revolyutsionnaya perestroika', *Pravda*, 26/11/1989.

Gorbachev, Mikhail (1991), *The August Coup: The Truth and the Lessons*, London: HarperCollins.

Hobsbawm, Eric (1992), *The Age of Revolution*, London: Weidenfeld & Nicolson.

Hopton, A. (ed.), **Winstanley, G.** (1989), *Selected Writings*, London: Aporia Press.

Horowitz, Irving (ed.) (1989), *Cuban Communism*, New York: Transaction Publishers, 7th edition.

Hudelson, R. (1993), *The Rise and Fall of Communism*, Boulder, CA: Westview Press.

Jackson, K.D. (ed.) (1989), *Cambodia 1975–78: Rendezvous with Death*, Princeton: Princeton University Press.

Johnson, Christopher (1974), *Utopian Communism in France: Etienne Cabet and the Karians*, Ithaca: Cornell University Press.

Joravsky, David (1994), 'Communism in historical perspective', *American Historical Review*, June 1994, 837–57.

Kaser, Michael (1967), *Comecon: Integrated Problems of the Command Economies*, Oxford: Oxford University Press.

Kelly, Catriona and **Shepherd, D.** (eds) (1998), *Constructing Russian Culture in the Age of Revolution 1881–1940*, Oxford: Oxford University Press.

Kennedy-Pipe, Caroline (1998), *Russia and the World 1917–91*, London: Arnold.

Khrushchev, Nikita (1971), *Khrushchev Remembers*, London: Little, Brown and Co.

Kolakowski, Leszek (1978), *Main Currents of Marxism*, Oxford: Clarendon Press.

Laqueur, Walter (1994), *The Dream that Failed*, Oxford: Oxford University Press.

Laslett, Peter (1988), *The World We Have Lost: Further Explored*, London: Routledge.

Lenin, Vladimir (1902), *What is to be Done?* Moscow: Progress Publishers, 1983.

Lenin, Vladimir (1920), 'Report of the All-Russia Central Executive Committee to the 8th Congress of Soviets', *Selected Works*, Moscow: Progress Publishers, 1967, vol. 3.

Lichtheim, George (1975), *A Short History of Socialism*, London: Fontana.

Marx, Karl (1845), 'The German ideology', in MECW, vol. 5, London: Lawrence and Wishart, 1976.

Marx, Karl (1864), 'Inaugural address of the Working Men's International Association', in MECW, vol. 20, London: Lawrence and Wishart, 1984.

Marx, Karl (1867), 'Capital', in MECW, vol. 35, London: Lawrence and Wishart, 1986.

Marx, Karl and Engels, Friedrich (1848), *The Manifesto of the Communist Party 1848*, Moscow: Progress Publishers, 1977.

Marx, Karl and Engels, Friedrich (1850), 'Address of the Committee to the Communist League', in MECW, vol. 10, London: Lawrence and Wishart, 1978.

Marx, Karl and Engels, Friedrich (1871), 'The Civil War in France', in MECW, vol. 22, London: Lawrence and Wishart, 1984.

Marx, Karl and Engels, Friedrich (1875), 'The Critique of the Gotha Programme', in MECW, vol. 24, London: Lawrence and Wishart, 1985.

More, Thomas (1989), *Utopia*, Cambridge: Cambridge University Press.

Nove, Alec (1992), *An Economic History of the USSR*, Harmondsworth: Penguin.

Okey, Robin (1982), *Eastern Europe 1740–1980*, London: Hutchinson.

Pipes, Richard (2002), *Communism*, London: Phoenix.

Ponchaud, F. (1978), *Cambodia Year Zero*, New York: Holt, Rinehart and Winston.

Read, Christopher (1990), *Culture and Power in Revolutionary Russia*, Basingstoke: Macmillan.

Rose, R.B. (1978), *Gracchus Babeuf: The First Revolutionary Communist*, London: Arnold.

Royle, E. (1998), *Robert Owen and the Commencement of the Millennium*, Manchester: Manchester University Press.

Saich, Tony (1981), *China: Politics and Government*, Basingstoke: Macmillan.

Saint-Simon, Henri de (1975), *Selected Writings on Science and Industry*, London: Croom Helm.

Sakwa, Richard (1999), *Postcommunism*, Milton Keynes: Open University Press.

Sandle, Mark (1996), 'The final word: the draft Party Programme of July/August 1991', *Europe–Asia Studies*, 48, 1996, 1131–50.

Sandle, Mark (1999), *A Short History of Soviet Socialism*, London: UCL Press.

Sandle, Mark (2002), 'Brezhnev and Developed Socialism: the ideology of zastoi?', in Bacon, Edwin and Sandle, Mark (eds), *Brezhnev Reconsidered*, Basingstoke: Palgrave.

Sassoon, Donald (1997), *One Hundred Years of Socialism: The West European Left in the Twentieth Century*, London: Fontana.

Schram, Stuart (1974), *Mao Tse-Tung*, Harmondsworth: Penguin.

Scott, John (1989), *Behind the Urals*, Bloomington: Indiana University Press.

Service, Robert (1985), *Lenin: A Political Life* [volume 1], Basingstoke: Macmillan.

Shenfield, Stephen (1987), *The Nuclear Predicament*, London: Routledge.

Somerville, K. (1986), *Angola: Politics, Economics, Society*, London: Pinter.

Stayer, J. (1994), *The German Peasants' War and the Anabaptist Community of Goods*, Montreal: McGill-Queen's University Press.

Stern, Geoffrey (1990), *The Rise and Decline of International Communism*, Aldershot: Edward Elgar.

Stites, Richard (1989), *Revolutionary Dreams*, Oxford: Oxford University Press.

Taubman, William (2002), *Khrushchev: The Man and his Era*, New York: W.W. Norton.

Taylor, Keith (1982), *The Political Ideas of the Utopian Socialists*, London: Cass.

Ulassi, P. (1969), 'Communism in Western Europe', in Jacobs, Dan (ed.), *The New Communisms*, New York: Harper and Row.

Utley, G. (2000), *Pablo Picasso: The Communist Years*, New Haven: Yale University Press.

Walicki, Andrzej (1995), *Marxism and the Leap to the Kingdom of Freedom: The Rise and Fall of the Communist Utopia*, Stanford: Stanford University Press.

Woodhouse, Michael and **Pearce, Brian** (1975), *Essays on the History of Communism in Britain*, London: New Park Publications.

Index